TREETOPS

TREETOPS

STORY OF A
WORLD FAMOUS HOTEL

R·J·Prickett

David & Charles
Newton Abbot   London   North Pomfret (Vt)

To
Gertrude Annie
who made all things possible

British Library Cataloguing in Publication Data

Prickett, R. J.
    Treetops: story of a world famous hotel.
    Treetops Hotel —— History
    I. Title
    647′.94676201′0924   TX 941.T

    ISBN 0–7153–9020–1

Phototypeset by ABM Typographics Limited Hull
and printed in Great Britain
by Butler & Tanner Limited Frome
for David & Charles Publishers plc
Brunel House   Newton Abbot   Devon

Published in the United States of America
by David & Charles Inc
North Pomfret   Vermont 05053   USA

CONTENTS

.The new Treetops was built in 1957, as soon as the Emergency was declared to be over. Water was pumped from the Muringato River to make the pool as big as this (*Block Hotels Archives*)

INTRODUCTION

To most people, the name 'Treetops' probably conjures up no more than a vague picture of a hut in a tree somewhere in Kenya, a Wendy house in a fig-tree where Princess Elizabeth became Queen Elizabeth II in 1952, and to the site of which she returned in 1983. Only a handful of people know of the other wonderful things that happened and they are getting fewer as the years roll by. The author of this book is one of them, having worked for eight years at Treetops, walked with Her Majesty for half a mile and talked with her for half an hour, and carried out more than a year of intensive research, interviewing more than fifty people and reading almost as many books.

In 1968 I left the service of the Kenya Government after twenty-two years as a Forester, including ten years as an Honorary Game Warden protecting crops and livestock from the ravages of elephants, buffaloes, lions and leopards. I had been given a golden handshake and requested to earn a living elsewhere, for Kenya, an independent country, had no further need of its British civil servants. With my wife, Gertrude Annie, I packed up and returned to the land of my birth but not the land of my choice, and tried hard to fit into a country that had been made alien by years of absence. After eight months, disillusioned and suffering from what has been called the 'Claws of Africa', I decided to make one final effort and find my true destiny. I bought a three-month return ticket to Kenya, leaving Gertrude Annie behind.

Arriving in Kenya I bought a battered old minibus or 'Kombi' as they were known at that time, and in this I lived between frantic searches up and down the country for employment. At last, with only a few days left on that three-month ticket (claiming a refund on the unused half is not possible after three months), and with little money left, I obtained a job as Assistant Hunter at Treetops on a three-month contract. The possibility that it would not thereafter be permanent never entered my head, and I forthwith sent a telegram to Gertrude Annie telling her the good news and asking her to join me as soon as possible. Within a week we were reunited at Nairobi Airport. The contract was not renewed, and for a short time two had to live in a minibus that had hardly appeared big enough for one.

When the chips are really down a man is very often at his best. There followed a period of about a year when the wolf was kept from the door by professional hunting, stints of work at various game-viewing lodges, and even six weeks looking after a cattle ranch whilst the owner was absent in England. Salvation came when I found employment as hunter at a newly built game-viewing lodge known as the Ark, a job which was to last eight years.

I was married on the ninth day of the ninth month in the year 1939. Gertrude Annie and I have ever since looked upon the figure nine as our lucky number. At the end of my three-month stint at Treetops, we left the Outspan Hotel, which is the base for it, on 31 March 1969. On 1 April 1978 we were back—exactly nine years later. There was nothing special in the coincidence. The job became vacant due to a retirement and I applied for the post and was accepted, but to Gertrude Annie and me it was a nine-year act of fate.

1
SETTING THE SCENE: NYERI AND KIKUYULAND

The land which forms the background of this book is some 5,000 square miles (13,000km²), stretching from Nairobi in the south to a much smaller town called Nanyuki in the north. Between, but much nearer Nanyuki, lies Nyeri, an administrative centre and a town of importance but with less than 30,000 inhabitants. The area is about 120 miles (190km) in length and 30 miles (50km) wide.

To the east towers the dominant feature of snow-clad Mount Kenya, flanked at the Nairobi end by the much lower Machakos Hills. To the west, running almost the full length, lie the Aberdare Mountains (the Nyandaruas), a range which actually forms a wall of the Great Rift Valley. The land between, mostly a broad valley, is some of the most fertile in Kenya.

Today it is known as Central Province, but this was not always so. In former times it was called simply Kikuyuland, and was feared by every explorer of the last century, because of the ferocity of the Wakikuyu tribe, the agricultural people who lived in the forest edges, and of the Maasai, who grazed their herds in the centre. On the southern flank were the Wakamba, of those Machakos Hills, fighting men who have been soldiers in the armies of colonisers and colonised alike, and through whose lands it was necessary to pass before reaching Kikuyuland. Another tribe, the Wandorobo, hunted deep in the forest as hunter-gatherers, but they were elusive people and harmed nobody.

Precisely when the Wakikuyu came to Kikuyuland is not known with certainty, for there are no written records, and researchers are not unanimous in their findings, but no date has been suggested earlier than 400 years ago. They are a Bantu people and are thought to have come from the Congo and Uganda. They were often in conflict with the Maasai, who

9

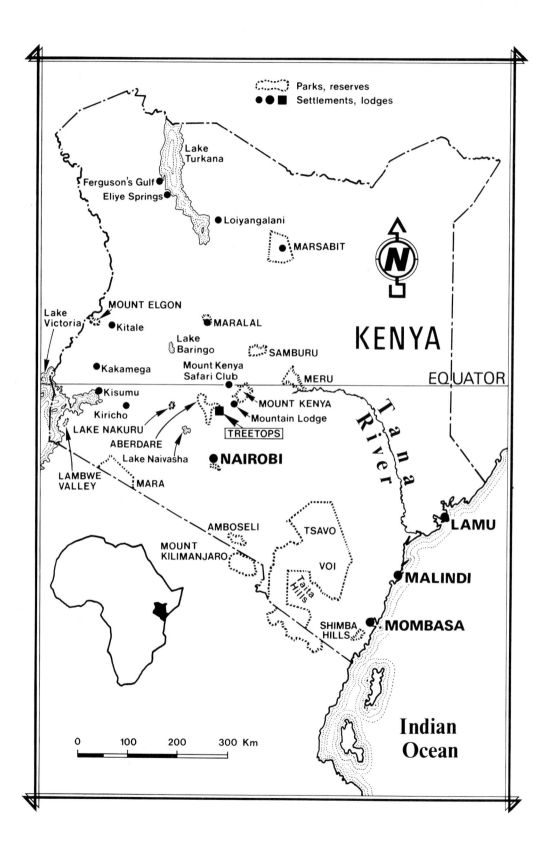

arrived a little later, moving southwards down the Great Rift Valley from the direction of the Sudan. Each of the two tribes took men and women as slaves from the other from time to time, resulting in intermarriage and duplication of customs. Both tribes agree that when their ancestors first arrived the land was inhabited by the Wandorobo, and that a more ancient tribe still, the Gumba, still existed in small numbers. The Gumba, a persecuted people, are now gone, though shards of pottery discovered high up on the Aberdares show that the inhospitable moorlands were their last refuge.

The Wakikuyu have always been agriculturists, practising a form of shifting cultivation well suited to a situation of small populations and vast forests. Fire and small axes were the chief tools of clearance, the *jembe* (hoe) and the *panga* (a form of machete) the chief tools of cultivation. Crops of *wimbi* and later maize and bananas were planted on the cleared forest land for a period of three or four years; then the cultivators moved on and cleared more forest, leaving nature to regenerate. Often an over-abundance of goats prevented this and the land merely became bush.

Count Teleki, describing his journey through Kikuyuland in 1887 relates how he saw great areas of newly felled trees, most of them charred and some of them still smoking, lying in disorder on the ground. There is little doubt that much virgin forest had been cleared in Kenya before the first Europeans arrived. The destruction was to increase vastly.

Wakikuyu villages were small in those days, groups of beehive-shaped huts in strips of forest deliberately left as escape routes to the main forests. Each hut would be connected to others by paths worn smooth by bare feet. The Wakikuyu greatly feared the raiding Maasai and had intricate systems of gates across the approach paths, covered pits containing pointed stakes, and ambush sites. The latter consisted of trenches overgrown with creepers in which warriors would hide. They also maintained twenty-four hour watches at vantage points around the village. When their enemies appeared the villagers simply melted into the main forest with all their cattle and goats, fighting a rearguard action with poisoned arrows and short-bladed spears, ideal for quick work amongst the trees. The Maasai were loath to follow far, for though they were a fearless match for lions on the plains they did not understand the forests, and both hated and feared them. The forests were dark and full of strange animals, deadly snakes and the spirits of dead Kikuyu.

The Maasai, a Nilotic tribe, moved south from the Sudan some three hundred years ago, bringing their vast herds of hump-backed Boran cattle with them. They moved down the rich grassland of the Great Rift Valley and circled the Aberdares from the direction of Lake Baringo. Warriors to the fingertips, they had no time for agriculture and despised the Wakikuyu, whose cattle they took as of right, for, in their eyes, all cows had been given to them and them alone by their god. The Maasai live on a diet consisting almost exclusively of milk and blood, (made to coagulate until almost like cheese), reserving meat for ceremonial occasions.

Just as there is a mystery about the remarkable health of the Maasai on their frugal diet of milk and blood so there is a mystery about their origins. Some researchers think there is the blood of the Lost Roman Legion in their veins, though the Maasai themselves scoff at the idea. Certainly there are features reminiscent of the Romans—the hairstyle, the heraldic patterns on their shields, the toga, the short sword, and the meetings of elders in a forum. They believe in themselves as God's chosen people— the sons of Engai—and their arrogance is that of the Roman warrior.

Though the language is Nilotic, the age-group system and the practices of circumcision and clitorectomy ('female circumcision'), the shaving of women's heads, and front-teeth extraction are Hamitic, as is the one-legged stance curled around a spear.

In the 300 years since they arrived in the area, the Maasai can trace through legend twelve *Loibons* or religious leaders, of which Olenana, Mbatiani and Nelion are the best known. Mbatiani died in 1889 and was famous for his prophesies. He foretold the epidemic of smallpox which was to decimate his people. He correctly prophesied the outbreak of rinderpest which left dead cattle everywhere and almost exterminated the vast herds of buffalo. But it was his prophesy of the coming of the railway from Mombasa to Kisumu on the shores of Lake Victoria that was the most remarkable. He said that an iron snake would wind across the country, that its head would be in one sea and its tail in another, and that along its body would be wooden boxes full of people all bellowing and crying—not a bad picture of a train for someone in a country where no train had yet been seen.

Of all primitive peoples the Maasai have clung with notably fierce determination to their old ways, and even today there are instances where highly educated men have returned to herding cattle. Nevertheless some are now becoming ranchers and some are growing wheat on their broad acres.

At the turn of the century the Maasai were still raiding the agricultural Wakikuyu for their cattle—and to take the best of their women as slaves— and looked upon it as a sport, for had not their god, Engai, given all cattle to them? They lived for fighting, and, looking at their spears and wooden

'Rift Valley' scenery taken by an unknown photographer about 1932. Maj Sherbrooke Walker travelled the dirt road on his way to Uganda in 1926. This land has now changed beyond recognition

knobkerries, would mutter 'Steel for the men—wood for the women and children'.

When, after World War I, the British were allocating land in this fertile area, they decided to form barriers of settlement between the two tribes. Later, they took away the Maasai shields, but as this left their cattle vulnerable to the many lions it did not work. Eventually an agreement was made with the Maasai chiefs to exchange lands at Narok and they all trekked out with their cattle.

Today all that remains in the land now called Central Province of the Maasai presence which featured so much in Her Majesty's memories of 1952 and again in 1983 are a few Maasai who remained as cattle-herders on some of the big ranches and the many place names. The highest peaks on Mount Kenya—Mbatian, Nelion and Lenana—are named after those three Maasai *Loibons,* and the three towns strung the length of the land— Nairobi, Nyeri and Nanyuki—also have Maasai names.

When the 'iron snake', the Kenya–Uganda railway, reached a halfway point, an uninhabited swamp was encountered. Quite apart from the problems of crossing it the workers needed a rest and a small encampment arose on the site. The Maasai knew the area of course, as they often watered their cattle there. They called it N'erobi, the place of cold waters. The railway arrived at what is now the city of Nairobi in May 1899.

At this time Nyeri did not exist, though caravans used to pass the site with merchandise destined for tribes living along the shores of Lake Victoria. Their path took them along the northern shoulder of the Aberdares and across the Laikipia Plains. Popular items of trade were buffalo hides to be used as war shields by the Kavirondo tribes.

In 1902 a caravan of traders was winding its way on foot, with mules and donkeys, when it was attacked by a band of Tetu warriors (the Tetu were an offshoot of the Wakikuyu tribe) and the traders were murdered to a man. When the British Government heard about the incident its reaction was swift and effective. It ordered to the site a small punitive force under the command of a Capt R. W. Meinertzhagen. After carrying out his task, he camped by a clear river (later to become known as the Chania River) at the foot of a wooded hill which the locals called Nyiri—a Maasai name meaning upside down. Meinertzhagen named the place—the site of the future town—after the hill. Researchers seem to think that the Maasai name must have referred to some tribal dancing action, but it is much more likely to refer to the shape of the hill. We know that the Maasai despised the Wakikuyu for the agricultural habits. A Kikuyu woman cultivating bends perfectly straight from the waist and her head is upside down. Nyeri Hill, viewed from certain angles, looks just like a Kikuyu woman cultivating.

Nanyuki, the last of the three towns strung along the length of Kikuyuland, lies at the foot of Mount Kenya, on the banks of the small Nanyuki river. Today Nanyuki has a big army base, and an airforce headquarters, and there are factories being built, but it still has a frontier atmosphere, for there is no other settlement of consequence before one reaches the borders of Ethiopia and Somalia more than 400 miles (640km) to the north.

During World War II one was entitled to the Africa Star the moment one's unit proceeded 'North of Nanyuki', for in addition to enemy action the local tribes lived by raiding, and soldiers who wandered were apt to just disappear. I remember Nanyuki as a single, red-earthed, dusty road whose *dukas* (Indian shops) lined each side and were roofed with either *mabati* (galvanised iron sheets), or flattened *debes*—4gal (18l) petrol tins in universal use at that time.

Ngare Nanyuki means in Maasai 'red river'. It is a crystal clear river for it runs straight off the snows of Mount Kenya, and much forest still clothes its banks. It was a place where the forest-dwelling Wakikuyu and the plains-loving Maasai met, and surely at some distant time in the past there must have been fighting which turned its clear waters red.

When the first European settlers arrived, in 1910, both the plains and the forests were alive with wild animals, and farming was a continual battle for survival. In spite of constant shooting little impression was made on the vast herds until the closing years of World War II, when 80,000 Italian prisoners of war had to be fed. I am glad I can remember the days when the plains were teeming with wildlife, the grandest spectacle on earth, but these memories are made bitter by others, of journeys made to the field butchery at Nanyuki when I saw row upon row of zebra, eland, hartebeest, oryx, and impala carcasses.

The third tribe in this part of the land so well known to Her Majesty is the Wandorobo, or Okiek, as the purists would have us call them, and they survive today only in the remote areas. Before the arrival of the Wakikuyu, and then the Maasai, they were undoubtedly hunter-gatherers of wild animals and honey in both the dense forests and the bush country. Whether the more primitive Gumba finally died out or intermarried is not known with certainty. What is known for sure is the fact that bushmanoids, and the related pygmies of the rain forests, occupied the whole of southern Africa and disappeared as their favoured forests retreated or were occupied by more warlike tribes.

Even as early as 1924 J. A. Massam, in his book *The Cliff Dwellers of Kenya,* describes how an old Dorobo was taken to court under laws introduced by the British for killing an elephant at Elgeyo. The author laments the fact that so many of these romantic people are leaving the forests and working outside, or intermarrying with other tribes.

Vivienne de Watteville, in her book *Out in the Blue,* vividly describes hunting bongo in the Aberdares during the same year, and how they were helped by the little forest dwellers, the Wandorobo, and their yellow dog called *rusapi.* This theme of Wandorobo tracking in the depths of the forests of Kenya is reiterated over and over again by the old-time hunters. One book recently published about the Wandorobo asserts that they number 21,000 people. This is simply not true. Robbed of their forests and their ancient way of life they have had no option but to disperse and intermarry. Yet they are the only tribe which left their habitat wholesome and pure—just as they found it.

As mentioned elsewhere, the Maasai despised the Wandorobo, who possessed no cattle but hunted in the forests for meat and honey. They called them *Il Torobo,* the poor people. Their legend is that once upon a time an Okiot (singular for Okiek) so annoyed their god Engai by killing cows instead of keeping them for milk and blood and breeding that he ordained that no more cows would be sent down from heaven for them and that henceforth the whole tribe would be condemned to hunt. Nevertheless the Maasai have in common with the Wandorobo circumcision rites and the practice of making trinkets of metal.

The Wakikuyu despised the Maasai because they did not till the soil. Malcontents from other tribes have, in the past, joined the Wandorobo in the forest to live a life free of tribal restraints, and this caused them to be classed as ne'er-do-wells by the early British. The true Wandorobo, however, is still a fine type, of a gentle disposition.

The true Wandorobo were a small people, as dwellers in forests usually are, be they elephants or men. They hunted with bows and arrows, and with the help of small yellow dogs, whose business was to bay up the larger beasts until the hunter arrived. Spears were not always used, as they are a hindrance to rapid movement in dense forests. Similarly poison was not always used on the arrows. The Wandorobo encouraged shrill barking by their dogs as a means to hold the animal at bay, but other tribes, notably the pygmies, used silent dogs with bells hung around each dog's waist. The Wandorobo set snares made of twisted bark, and sometimes of the skins of the animals themselves. They also used drop spears, triggered by a twisted-creeper rope. And of course they constantly collected honey.

Honey barrels were, and still are, a major source of collected honey for the Wandorobo and their construction occupied much of their time. The barrels are made from the two halves of a log, hollowed out and bound tight with creepers. Collecting honey from a number of widely scattered barrels slung high in trees is looked upon as one of the most important tasks of the day. Forest antelopes are hunted as the collectors wander from barrel to barrel.

The houses of the Wandorobo, once found deep within the forests themselves but now invariably on the outskirts, are low and shaped rather like those of the Maasai. They are never, however, made of mud and dung like the Maasai huts, presumably because of the lack of cattle to provide the dung, but are of long withies from the forest bent over and interlaced with leaves.

The first serious set back to the lifestyle of the Wandorobo in Kenya came about when vast areas of forest were gazetted by the Government as Forest Reserves under the administration of the Forest Department. The first Reserves came into being in the early days of the present century; the

The Ngong Hills site of the ill-fated hunting lodge given by the settlers of Kenya to Princess Elizabeth and the Duke of Edinburgh as a wedding present. A last minute decision by the then Governor of Kenya switched the site to Mount Kenya

last were not completely taken over until after World War II. Forest laws subsequently passed not only made it an offence to hunt within these gazetted forests but made it illegal even to live there. A solution had to be found to the problem of the Wandorobo.

Eventually two areas were set aside exclusively for the Wandorobo, one each side of the Great Rift Valley. Olengurone was the place 'West of Rift' in the Mau forests and all Wandorobo as far as Mount Elgon were persuaded to take up land. They could still go into the Forest Department areas on special licence to put up their honey barrels, paying a small due for each barrel, but they could not legally hunt there and they could not stay overnight. A similar area known as 'East of Rift' was set aside and known as the Mukagodo. The Wandorobo from the Aberdares and from Mount Kenya could take up land there, with the right to put out honey barrels on the two mountain masses.

The final eclipse of the Wandorobo tribe as a hunter-gatherer people came about a few years later with the outbreak of Mau Mau. From 1952 until 1957 the Forest Reserves of Mount Kenya, the Aberdares, the Mau, Mount Londiani and Lembus, and Mount Elgon were declared closed areas. Those who were seen by patrols and did not surrender immediately could be shot. On Mount Kenya and the Aberdares the dropping of heavy bombs on suspected Mau Mau camps became a daily occurrence. It was during those Mau Mau years that I met two Wandorobo deep in the forest, and it was an experience never likely to occur again.

The year was 1956. I had left Kenya with my army unit at the end of World War II but I had become a Forester and had just been seconded back to Mariashoni in the Southwest Mau Forest Reserve. Mau Mau was very much a dying force in the field, though sweeps were still being made in the forests and occasionally men were being killed or captured. There was still a tense feeling in what was then Kenya Colony. A number of Forest Stations had been closed and plantations had not been visited for four long years. I had only just arrived from England a few days before, and the Kenya of those days was very different from the Kenya I had known as a soldier during the war. It was all very new and very confusing. My first assignment, in a forest that had just opened, was to go out every day and find and report on these plantations. I was accompanied by two Forest Guards. They were armed with a spear, a bow and arrow or just the universal machete, always a part of a Forest Guard's uniform. Sometimes we found the plantations damaged by wild animals, by man or by fire. Sometimes we did not find them at all, for tropical growth in four years is formidable.

On this particular morning, after tramping some 5 miles (8km) along game paths in the forest, we encountered two Wandorobo in the full regalia of their traditional hunting dress. This was not the simple blanket so often described by writers who confused them with the Maasai. They were dressed in the skins of the animals of the forest. The two Forest Guards greeted them with handshakes and words in a language I could not understand; many of the Forest Guards of those days were of Wandorobo origin themselves, and it was obvious that the four were not strangers. Certainly they were not the dreaded Mau Mau that I had been warned to watch out for, though, had we been a security patrol, they might well have been shot on sight, with questions asked later. Only a few weeks afterwards, and not many miles away, at Elburgon, an old man from the Forest Village who had been visiting an abandoned *shamba,* or cultivated area, for food, was shot and killed by a patrol. I do not doubt for a moment that those two Forest Guards protected the two Wandorobo by warning them of impending security patrols, and I do not doubt they received a leg of venison from time to time for the favour.

How I wish I could remember clearly just how those two were dressed. They were as identical as twins, small, and thin featured. On their heads they both wore pointed fur caps of what I now know would be hyrax skins. Their earlobes held small coloured beads. Their jackets and their shorts were of bush-buck doe-skin, with the russet-brown hair pointing smoothly down. In the left hand they each carried a small bow with its notched arrow. A full bamboo quiver was slung over the shoulder. They also carried a bag made of a darker skin, probably that of the male bush-buck. All that land will be under plantations today, for it was eventually earmarked to provide cypress and pine for the huge Webuye Paper Mills.

With the departure of the Maasai and the Wandorobo the Wakikuyu multiplied and prospered. They had worked on the farms of the Europeans and in Nairobi offices, and, being a very clever people, had advanced much faster than the tribes living elsewhere. Today, however, the Government of Kenya discourages tribalism other than the keeping alive of the dress, the dances and the songs. Citizens are urged to think of themselves first and foremost as Kenyans, rather than as members of a particular tribe. Having described the people we now move to that wonderful mountain dominating the land, which, on clear days, can be seen from Nairobi, 100 miles (160km) to the south as the vulture flies.

Mount Kenya, or Kirinyaga to the Wakikuyu, means 'The mountain of splendour'. It was first seen by Western eyes on 3 December 1849, when the missionary explorer Dr Ludwig Krapf, standing on a hill above the Wakamba village of Kitui, saw the twin peaks through a break in the clouds. It was a few minutes before sunset. In spite of the distance and the fact that it was only revealed for a few minutes he was able to describe it in detail to an unbelieving world upon his return to Europe. Although he stayed in the area for some weeks he did not see it again.

Krapf was so upset by the scepticism about his reports that he returned in 1851, and even went 40 miles (65km) nearer but still failed to see his snow-covered mountain again. His caravan was then attacked and scattered by a raiding party of Wakamba tribesmen, and he was compelled to return to the coast, having failed in his objective. Note that he did not go to Nairobi, which in 1851 was but a place name identifying for Maasai herdsmen somewhere where they could water cattle.

Mount Kenya was not again seen by a European until 1883, when Joseph Thomson, travelling the Laikipia Plateau, saw its western face from a point much nearer. He was a scientist as well as an explorer, and he was able to explain to a now more attentive Western world that Mount Kenya was an ancient and extinct volcano whose crater had been worn away, and that the peaks were of magma that had fallen in like a plug which 'closed the volcanic life of the mountain'. We are told today not only that this graphic description was true but that Mount Kenya was originally nearly as high as present-day Everest.

In October 1887 Count Teleki, a wealthy Hungarian nobleman, ascended Mount Kenya to an altitude of 15,355ft (4,680m) and the valley up which he climbed bears his name today. In 1899 Mount Kenya was successfully scaled for the first time. In that year Sir Halford Mackinder climbed the peak Batian (17,058ft/5,199m). Not until 1929, thirty years later, was the slightly lower peak Nelion (17,022ft/5,188m) conquered by Eric Shipton. Nelion, incidentally, was the brother of the Maasai *Loibon* Mbatiani. Over the years more than thirty people have lost their lives attempting to climb this treacherous mountain.

Because Mount Kenya sits astride the Equator it enjoys what is called an Afro-Alpine climate; and because of long hours of intense sunshine in a rarified atmosphere, combined with a very high rainfall, it produces a range of gigantic plants which are both beautiful and unique. Above 10,000ft (3,050m) and below the scree line of 12,000ft (3,650m), vast areas of giant heather, tall enough to screen whole herds of elephants, make islands in the sea of waving brown tussock grass. Isolated groups of hagenia trees, often called East African rosewood, stand festooned with the lichen Old Man's Beard. On the sweet green grass growing below these trees lurk suni, the smallest of all the East African antelopes, little larger than a rabbit. They look like elves and gnomes in fairyland.

Groups of giant lobelias stand sentinel in the marshes, looking from a distance like an army that never moves, and on the rockier ground giant groundsel, towering 20ft (6m) above the ground, sometimes display masses of glorious golden flowers that gladden the heart. A little lower, where it is not quite so cold at night, fields of Everlasting Daisies (*Helichrysum*) cover a land that has known the impact of no human hand, and carpet the ground with white and pink. Here and there stand groups of salmon-pink gladioli waving in the breeze like daffodils in Europe. Very, very rarely a deep-purple orchid stands like some exotic candle in the grass.

There are patches too of Red-Hot Pokers, the wild cousins of those seen in gardens. Even nettles and thistles are bigger than those seen elsewhere, and on path edges, where buffalo have grazed and fertilised the soil, the clover is not white but a glorious purple.

Before descending to the zone of Alpine bamboo, clumps of sugar bush can be found, a plant with rose-like flowers of a rich gold colour, but without any thorns. The bamboo zone, starting at an altitude of 9,000ft (2,750m) and ending on the moorlands with dwarf clumps no more than 1yd (0.9m) high, is a mysterious world of its own, where, in the fertile soil of valleys, the tangled culms tower more than 40ft (12m), sway and groan with every ploy of wind, and are dripping wet for most of the year, for they create and harbour the mists. Cold, damp and misty, the bamboo forests contain little wildlife, and—like the pine forests of Europe—could be described as botanical wildernesses. Nevertheless their lonely recesses have always been a refuge for animals with young, and for animals over-hunted outside. The lower contours of Mount Kenya contain (or at least they did in the days of my hunting there—not so long ago) wonderful stands of cedar, podo, camphor and Meru oak.

The Aberdares are a range whose two high points are much lower than Mount Kenya. Sattima at the northern end is 13,120ft (4,000m) and Kinangop to the south is 12,815ft (3,906m). Snow showers have been recorded but they never lie on the ground. It is commonly said that the Aberdares are the eastern wall of the Great Rift Valley, but Dr Celia Nyamweru, in her wonderful book *Rifts and Volcanoes*, maintains that this is an oversimplification of a very complex geological phenomenon. The Aberdare Range is but a part of what is known as the Afro-Arabian Rift System, a depression running 4,000 miles (6,400km) from Turkey to Mozambique (Maputo). The section in Africa is called the East African Rift System, and the part near Nairobi is the Gregory Rift Valley.

Rifting started more than 30 million years ago, but the forces which finally resulted in the present-day Rift are extremely complex, and are still at work. Between 5 million and 6½ million years ago, eruptions built up a wall of basalt lava which is the present-day Aberdare Range and nearby Ngong Hills, but some 3 million years later occurred what is called the Sattima Fault, which obliterated the various vents by a form of tilting.

The Aberdares were discovered to the Westerm world by the explorer Joseph Thomson in 1883 (see page 19), and he named them after Lord Aberdare, who had sponsored his expedition.

The total area of the range is about a thousand square miles, of which a third, mostly the upper reaches, are National Park and the remainder Forest Reserve or under cultivation. Treetops is situated at the extreme tip of a long tongue of forest stretching towards Mount Kenya and known as the Treetops Salient. This salient has been used from time immemorial as a migration route for animals travelling between the Aberdares and Mount Kenya. Today coffee, tea, and other valuable crops are grown here, and such migrations are almost impossible because of the electric fencing.

It will be recalled that Nyeri was not even a place name in 1902, and that Meinertzhagen named it after Nyeri Hill, at whose foot he had camped after his expedition against the Tetu. He was so enamoured of the site that he decided to build there a *boma* to station a few troops. A *boma* was originally, in the Kiswahili language, simply a ring of cut thorn bushes, where cattle and other domestic animals could sleep in safety at night. From that simple beginning *bomas* developed into much more effective enclosures built by warrior tribes, and, later, by soldiers of various nationalities at war. Soon *bomas* became more in the nature of stockades, the posts of which were normally cut from whatever species of tree were to hand. When this happened to be fig the posts usually struck, and eventually became a living wall.

Some of the fig-trees of the original Nyeri *boma* of 1902 can still be seen, though the building of the new provincial-government offices has destroyed most of them. Today, when we are going into Nyeri, we call out to our servants that we are 'going into town'. This is a comparatively new expression. Throughout our Forestry Department days it was: 'We are going to the *Boma*.'

In 1904, only two years after Meinertzhagen's punitive expedition, an Indian bazaar was operating in Nyeri, and by 1906 other traders were moving in, amongst them Sandy Herd, a European. He opened a store, housed in rondavels, grandiose replicas of the African's round huts, and a few years later the White Rhino came into being, Nyeri's first hotel. About the same time came a police station and, of course, a prison. By 1910 both a District Commissioner and a Forester had come to Nyeri. Between them they created a golf club, now called simply Nyeri Club. Its saga will be told in another chapter.

In 1909 the Church of Scotland Mission had been built at nearby Tumu Tumu and settlers were beginning to farm. Not until after World War I, however, did the land show any great change. Even when work commenced on the Outspan Hotel in 1926 the European population of the *boma* of Nyeri still numbered only nine. By 1930, however, Nyeri was being called, in the *East African Year Book,* a 'rising township'.

The beautiful tall avenue of Australian blue gums (eucalyptus trees) along Baden-Powell Road was planted in 1928 and 1929 by Jaswaran Singh Sehmi, whose son, Vir Singh Sehmi runs the Aberdare Timber Company. Some of the trees are now over 150ft (45m) tall, but they are shallow rooted. Many have fallen down during storms, and many others have now been felled because they are a hazard to traffic. There are many beautiful flowerings trees in Kenya and doubtless some day the avenue will be restored.

Besides being important to this book because it is the seat of the administration of Central Province, Nyeri is important to me because it is my home.

In 1971, when I was out of a regular job and doing almost anything to keep the wolf from the door, my wife Gertrude Annie and I lived in a tiny stone cottage in Nanyuki, paying the princely rental of £15 a month. Cheap as it was, there were months when we were hard put to find the rent. What was worse, however, was the fact that the Asian owner wanted us out. He wanted to sell it and leave the country. We did not want to stay, for there were huge cracks in the walls and the floors. It was then that we heard that a house was for sale in Nyeri, and one day we went to see it.

The stone house, built by Baron Poltimore in 1943, stood but a few hundred yards from the Outspan Hotel. The Outspan had been virtually rebuilt and very much extended in the same year as the house was built, and the same grey stones and red tiles had been used in both buildings. Baron Poltimore was eccentric. He wanted his wife at what he considered the right distance—the other end of the house. Accordingly, each end was self-contained with its own bedroom and bathroom. Only the central lounge and dining-room were communal. There were servants aplenty. In the 3½ acre (1.5ha) garden he erected huge wired-in enclosures to grow plenty of fruit and vegetables, all of which he then gave away. When the Baron died, alone and without relatives, the Public Trustees took over the property. They let it stand empty for seven years before putting it up for sale.

There is little doubt that Baron Poltimore, in his later years, neglected the estate, and this, added to the seven years' lack of upkeep by the Public Trustees, produced a wilderness it is hard to describe. We had to battle our way up the drive to reach the front door. When we entered we had to push our way through a curtain of cobwebs, and we found there was a hole in the roof where a tile had cracked and never been replaced. A section of ceiling had then collapsed, and a dead bat lay on a parquet floor so deep in dust we did not even know it was wood at the time.

Our prospects for the future were then much brighter, and, with the promise of a big bank loan, and a prayer in our hearts, we bought Baron Poltimore's sadly neglected house. Today, after years of hard work, there is no longer a bank loan, and the bungalow has been restored to its old splendour.

The grey stones and the red tiles were generally in perfect condition. Nyeri stone is really volcanic ash spewed out of Mount Kenya aeons ago and buried under tons of rubble; the resulting pressure has produced a 'welded tuff' harder than sandstone. It is considered to be the best building material in the country. Vandals and robbers had broken in over the years and removed anything of value that could be removed, including some of the best stonework in the garden. The highest and furthermost section of the garden had been used as a dumping ground for all who had something to dump. It boasted a number of car chassis and pieces of broken machinery including a maize-grinding machine. Only at this point could Mount Kenya be seen; so I dug a pit, broke up the derelict ironwork as far as possible, deposited it therein; then I added soil and finally retaining walls and steps, and ended up with a 6ft (1.8m) high structure from which I could clearly see the mountain whenever I wished. My staff called it my 'table'.

When I bought my 3½ acre (1.5ha) piece of wilderness in Nyeri in 1971, with its cobweb-festooned house in the middle, there was considerably more wildlife in the vicinity than there is today. Two grey duiker had taken up their abode in a particularly dense patch of cover, and I was really sorry when all the disturbance finally caused them to leave. One morning, soon after dawn, our gardener saw a beautiful leopard cross our land, and I myself saw its footprints a little later.

During the awful drought in 1984 some of the wildlife came back. I was walking up the drive at 8am one morning when a lovely duiker sprang out of a flower-bed near me. I rejoiced to think it had found both much-needed food and a safe refuge. A little later a porcupine ate up all the potato patch, and I tried hard to be as sympathetic.

Even today I can lie abed and listen to the raucous cries of the bush-babies in the trees of my own garden, and the more distant croaks of tree hyraxes in the Chania River valley. It is then I am so glad I live in Nyeri, and my thoughts echo the words of Lord Baden-Powell: 'The nearer to Nyeri the nearer to bliss.'

2

THE OUTSPAN HOTEL

The Outspan Hotel and Treetops were built by Maj Eric Sherbrooke Walker and his wife Lady Bettie. Much of this chapter is concerned with the lives of people who have lived either at the Outspan or in the vicinity, and these have included many famous people indeed. Today the Outspan Hotel is everything that is modern and progressive in the hotel industry, and, at the time of writing, is scheduled for further expansion. It has seventy-three beds, a fine swimming-pool, tennis courts, golfing arrangements with the nearby course, fishing in the Chania River, and facilities for conferences (very much a feature of Kenya today) of up to sixty people. The saga of how it all started can best be told by describing the life of Eric Sherbrooke Walker himself.

In 1908 Lord Baden-Powell, who spent his last years at the Outspan, and whose career is described later, appointed Walker as his first Scout Commissioner and his private secretary, appointments the latter held until the outbreak of World War I.

Walker joined the Royal Flying Corps and was shot down by the Germans over Europe and captured. From his prison camp he contacted B-P (as Lord Baden-Powell was known to his friends) by a secret code they shared, and, as a result, received from him wire-cutters in a ham bone. With these he escaped but he was recaptured. He escaped from other camps too, but never succeeded in crossing the border into nearby Holland where he would have been safe. As a result of learning Russian from fellow prisoners he was, in later years, able to put this knowledge to good use when he was sent to south Russia to work for military intelligence, and he served with the White Russians until they were finally defeated by the Bolsheviks. In his books he has a lot to say about the excitements of this period.

There is probably no-one else in the world who is entitled to wear the

The Outspan Hotel in 1987 offers such leisure pursuits as golf, swimming, fly fishing, tennis and squash

Military Cross, the Order of St Anne and the Order of St Stanislaus, together with the stars and ribbons of two world wars. It must have been extremely difficult for such a man to settle into civilian life again, and there followed a period in which the search for excitement pushed him on the wrong side of the law. This story is told in his book, written under the name of James Barbican, *Confession of a Rum Runner*. Walker records that he made a lot of money but that his involvement with a dishonest partner meant that he lost it almost as quickly. He also states, maybe with tongue in cheek, that he needed the money to get married.

The lady of his choice was Lady Bettie Feilding, daughter of the Earl of Denbigh, who he had first met when she had been only seven. There is little doubt that the marriage was a turning-point in Eric Sherbrooke Walker's life, for Lady Bettie proved to be a staunch and shrewd companion in his turbulent life.

In 1926 the Sherbrooke Walkers, low in funds, decided to leave England, and chose East Africa rather than New Zealand after a chance conversation informed them about its abundant wildlife. After a long sea journey they duly arrived at Mombasa, and stayed a while with Judge Sheridan before putting all their effects into bond and taking a train to Nairobi. In Nairobi they bought a new box-body Chevrolet car for the then princely sum of £240 and in this decided to tour Uganda's shocking roads in search of a suitable farm or ranch. They quickly discovered that they had not the money for such a venture, and soon the so-called roads of red soil became so bad that they were always digging themselves out or wondering if they were even on the road at all or merely a cattle-trail.

It was during this Uganda safari that their decision to build a hotel somewhere was made. They had spent the night in a hotel of such a low standard that they had both felt that, ignorant as they were of the hotel industry, they could hardly do worse. Apparently there were so many open knot-holes in the crude wooden walls of their bedroom that they had to drape towels over them before daring to undress for bed. The search henceforth was not for a farm but for a site for a hotel.

They then moved back into Kenya, and found their Shangri-La at Nyeri, 100 miles (160km) north of Nairobi, on roads that were just a tiny bit better than those they had experienced in Uganda. There is no record of where they stayed in Nyeri. Probably it was at the White Rhino Hotel, built by the Sandy Herd, Lord Cranworth and Hon Berkley Cole partnership from that early mud-and-wattle rondavel complex of the earlier days of the century.

During the following days the District Commissioner took the Sherbrooke Walkers along the banks of the Chania River searching for a suitable site for a hotel, and eventually they came to an open scrubby area looking down over the gorge. This area is a sloping tableland between two valleys, that of the Chania and another containing no water but debouching from the foothills of the Aberdares. It faced the glittering snows of Mount Kenya and was backed by the 40 mile (64km) Aberdare Range. The site was close enough to the river to present no problems pumping water, and so they decided that it must at last be the site for their dream hotel. Like much of Kenya at that time, the land was classified as Crown Land, coming directly under the administration of the District Commissioner. They bought an area of approximately 70 acres (30ha) from him, and started building almost at once.

A study of photographs almost sixty years old shows that the land on that ridge was indeed barren. Today, the planting of hundreds of trees, many of them flowering trees such as the exotic jacaranda and the indigenous flame tree has meant that, at certain times of the year, Nyeri is a blaze of colour—blue or red. It is interesting to note the words of Sherbrooke Walker: ' . . . it had never been inhabited by Man, and there was no question of depriving indigenous people of their land'. In 1926 the total population of Kenya was less than 3 million people.

The Outspan Hotel, Nyeri on opening day, New Year's Day 1928. (*Block Hotel Archives*)

So they built their embryo hotel, with the help of money borrowed from a benevolent bank manager. It was of local stone, and each of its four bedrooms had its own private bath and running water, a feature almost unheard of in the Kenya of 1926, where 'long drops' were dug at the bottom of the garden, the use of which, especially at night, was an adventure often involving chasing away unwelcome snakes. Even Nairobi, in 1926, had only its 'lavender cart' sanitation, operating at dead of night.

By the end of 1927 the Walkers had ten rooms, officially opened to the public on New Year's Day 1928, and it is recorded that expatriates came from far and near just for the nostalgic experience of pulling a chain in the water closets and hearing running water. A bottle of champagne was offered as a prize to anyone who could suggest a suitable name for the new hotel, and it was won by one of their friends, a saw-miller, Grace Barry, who suggested 'The Outspan', meaning the place where the traveller 'outspans' (unharnesses) his weary oxen at the end of the day, in contrast to 'inspanning', which took place when the journey started at dawn. This was a reference to those intrepid Boers of South Africa who travelled vast distances by ox cart, the *voortrekkers* of history.

During World War II Sherbrooke Walker subtracted fifteen years from his true age to enlist in the Royal Air Force, and tried to become a tail-gunner but never became airborne. He was transferred to the South African Division, then stationed in Kenya, and became a Divisional Intelligence Officer on Kenya's Northern Frontier, a vast, almost desert area. When the Advance came, in February 1941, he moved up with the

Division into Abyssinia (now Ethiopia), and finally on to the Western Desert, where, at Sidi Rezegh, his unit was surrounded by the Germans and he was almost captured once more.

The story of the building of Treetops in 1932 is a saga which will be told in the next chapter. During the Mau Mau Emergency Walker was running a farm at Naro Moru, about 30 miles (48km) away, where he spent his time when not involved with the Outspan. In his book *Treetops Hotel* he tells some hair-raising stories of those terrible days.

In 1961 the Sherbrooke Walkers sold both the Outspan and Treetops to the conservationist and philanthropist Sir Malin Sorsbie, who in 1966 sold out to Block Hotels Ltd.

For some years the Sherbrooke Walkers stayed on in Kenya, running their farm at Naro Moru. They then left and settled in Mallorca, where Eric died in 1976 at the age of eighty-five. Lady Bettie died in 1982 at the age of eighty-four. The death of Lady Bettie occurred only a few days before the fiftieth anniversary of Treetops, a day of great rejoicing tinged with regret for only the handful of people who had known its founders.

Although I did not see the Outspan Hotel until 1960 I did see the White Rhino in 1941. It looks very much the same today as it did then, and must be about the only building in Nyeri to have remained unchanged through more than half a century. After the Abyssinian campaign, I managed a seventy-two-hour leave from my unit then stationed outside Nairobi. My destination by train (nobody travelled by road at that time if it could be avoided) was the farm of a Capt Kenealy at Naro Moru. More will be told about that hectic leave when I describe Her Majesty's visit to the nearby church in 1952.

Capt Pat Kenealy, known affectionately to all and sundry as Kenealy Pat, because, as he was Irish, things had to be different, was in need of a new shirt because approximately half of his sunburnt torso was visible through the one he was wearing. At least his wife maintained that he was in need of a new shirt, but he himself insisted that he could never really be happy until a shirt was in the state of the one he was wearing and that would very soon be the fate of the new one but that, if she insisted, he was prepared to travel the 30 miles (48km) to Nyeri and buy a new one.

It thus came about that the three of us went to Nyeri in a box-body Ford car of ancient vintage along a road a foot deep in dust and with wild animals staring at us all the way. We had lunch at the White Rhino. Today, forty years later, two of our greatest African friends are running the place.

Nyeri town, in 1941, consisted of a single dusty red earthen road flanked

THE OUTSPAN HOTEL,

NYERI, KENYA COLONY.

The "Outspan" stands in its own grounds of 70 acres, with the Chania river flowing through them. The site was chosen for its cool, pleasant climate, its views of Kenya and the Aberdare Mountains, while the buildings were planned for comfort as the chief object.

Electric light; continual hot and cold water laid on; refrigerator; garage with English mechanic attached to hotel.

Golf-course adjoining hotel grounds; trout fishing; most kind of wild animals and big game within easy reach of the hotel. Good bird shooting.

No mosquitoes, no fever, and a healthy climate closely resembling that of a fine September in Scotland.

96 miles from Nairobi; hotel car meets every train at Nyeri station. (Trains leave Nairobi at 10 a.m. on Mondays, Wednesdays, and Fridays.)

In the township there are Post Office, Telegraph Office, European and Indian stores, another hotel ("The White Rhino"), C. of E. and R.C. Churches.

Modern Sanitation—English Baths.

TARIFF.

ROOMS.

Telegrams.

"Double suite."	Double bedroom, with verandah, private bath-dressing room and lavatory, fire, early tea. Per diem for two people	18/-
"Single suite."	Ditto, for one person ...	14/-

(To be opened January 14th, 1928.)

"Double room."	Double bedroom and early tea, for two people ...	13/-
"Single room."	Ditto, for one person ...	6/50

(To be opened in April, 1928.)

MEALS.

Breakfast. 3/50. Lunch, 3/50. Tea, 1/50. Dinner, 6/50.

En Pension.

	Per Day.	Per Week.	Per Month
Double suite, for two people; per person ..	21/50	128/-	450/-
Ditto, for one person	26/50	157/-	555/-
Double room, per person	19/-	113/-	395/-
Single room	19/-	113/-	395/-

Special terms to R.E.A.A.A. Members.

As the accommodation is limited at present, intending visitors are advised to send a reply paid telegram to make reservations.

NYERI, January, 1928.

E. A. Standard, Ltd.

on either side by *dukas* (small Asian shops), and in one of them the shirt was duly bought. It was run by Asians wearing their traditional dress of skullcap and flowing white robes, and on the counter was a packet of Camel cigarettes, a box of matches, a bottle of soft drink with its opener to hand, and an ancient newspaper. Two hard stools were positioned near-by. This hospitality was typical of Kenya of 1941. In spite of the war and its shortages, life went on very much in its old dreamy way. The incidental generosity did not alter the fact that hard bargaining had to be carried out before the shirt could be purchased, and all settlers maintained that Asians were crooks who prospered at their expense. It was quite true that they ran the commercial side of the country, but it was also true that they ran it very efficiently.

The dry valley that the Walkers saw in 1926 is today an extension of the golf course. The side facing Mount Kenya, however, is virtually covered with red-roofed bungalows on one-acre (1.2ha) plots. The other bank has been extensively planted with cypress and pines and very little of its original bush remains. The gorge of the Chania River, however, still con-tains a considerable amount of natural forest. There is still good fishing, but the river itself is now turbid, and everywhere along the banks are signs of illegal cultivation.

Trout were brought into Kenya in 1905 by Col Ewart Grogan. After an epic journey by sea to Mombasa, and then by train and road, they were released high up in the Aberdares. At that time there were no fish-eating tribes anywhere in the vicinity, and so the trout were never poached. Today there is an awareness of trout as a source of food, and it is doubtful if trout of the 10–12lb (4.5–5.5kg) class will ever be caught in Kenya again.

Many famous people have lived at the Outspan since Walker made that momentous decision to be a hotelier after his unfortunate night in Uganda, but none have left Nyeri such a legacy as Lord Robert Stephenson Smyth Baden-Powell, Baron of Gilwell, OM, GCMG, GCVO, KCB, founder of the Boy Scout movement and of the Girl Guides but just 'B-P' to his friends. In 1920 he was proclaimed Chief Scout of the World by the scouts who gathered in London for the first 'jamboree'. His wife, Lady Olave, was proclaimed Chief Girl Guide.

Lord Baden-Powell was born on 22 February 1857 and died on 8 January 1941, only a few days short of his eighty-fourth birthday. He was a brilliant general during the Boer War, and took part in the siege of Mafeking (a town in the northern part of South Africa), an event which earned him the extra title of 'Hero of Mafeking'. The siege lasted 217 days. I did not know Lord Baden-Powell, for he died just before the opening of the

Abyssinian Campaign. I did, however, meet Lady Olave, who survived him by many years, who was not only still the Chief Girl Guide but President of the Nyeri Branch of the East African Women's League.

Lord Baden-Powell first visited Kenya in 1906. Besides his other proficiencies he was both an artist and a writer, and it was in 1907 that he published his first book, *Sketches in Mafeking and East Africa.* In 1935 Lord and Lady Baden-Powell returned to Kenya together to carry out inspections of scouts at various rallies up and down the country, and it was then that B-P decided to visit his old friends the Sherbrooke Walkers at the hotel they had built in Nyeri. He fell in love with the Outspan at once, and when, two years later, his doctor ordered him to take a complete rest, it was to the Outspan that he came. He decided to make his last home there. In his own much quoted phrase: 'The nearer to Nyeri the nearer to bliss.'

So Sherbrooke Walker built for the Baden-Powells a special small cottage, and they came to live there in October 1938. The naming of that cottage is a romance in itself. The English home of the Baden-Powells at Bentley, Hampshire, purchased on Armistice Day at the end of World War I, had appropriately been 'Pax Hill'. B-P wanted his new cottage in Nyeri to be Pax too. When he disovered that in the Kiswahili language of East Africa the word for 'only' is *tu* he decided that, for a place of complete peace, 'Paxtu' it would have to be.

During the three years Lord Baden-Powell lived in 'Paxtu' he wrote a number of books: *Birds and Beasts of Africa, Paddle Your Own Canoe* and *More Sketches of Kenya.* He died in 1941 but his Scout Movement lives on, and each 22 February the mile-long road from the Outspan to the little church is crowded with thousands of Boy Scouts and Girl Guides of many races, marching and remembering. His grave faces Mount Kenya, and beside it are others, belonging to soldiers who died during the Mau Mau period and to settlers, some of whom also died during those terrible times; the graves of others bear the legend 'Killed by Elephant', 'Killed by Rhino' or 'Killed by Buffalo'.

In 1946 the Scouts and Guides of Kenya subscribed towards a memorial seat in the garden of 'Paxtu', to a signboard at the entrance and to a cedar plaque on the wall of the cottage itself. In July 1973 the twenty-fourth World Scout Conference took place in Kenya, the first in Africa. On that day a third-generation Lord Baden-Powell, grandson of B-P, visited the Outspan, 'Paxtu', and the grave holding the body of Lord Baden-Powell and the ashes of Lady Baden-Powell. 'Paxtu' is almost a shrine today, visited by people from all over the world. It has a sitting-room with a large verandah, two bedrooms, two bathrooms and two fireplaces and its own garden with birdbath and bird-table. It was no doubt ideal for B-P to concentrate on his last writings and paintings. It is now decorated in the Scout colours of blue and gold, and in the living-room are memorabilia of his life. Over the mantelpiece is a framed copy of his last Christmas card, of 1940, designed by himself and sent to his many friends all over the world. It was the darkest Christmas of the war. On it his message was: 'Have courage in the face of war, and fight on for better days of peace, to be enjoyed.' There is a copy of a letter sent to his secretary Eileen Wade about a recent safari in Kenya, and a glass cabinet contains various cards and copies of his books.

In 1960 I was posted from Kakamega in Western Kenya to a Forest Station 12 miles (20km) from Nyeri and about 1,000ft (300m) higher up the Aberdares. The name of Kiandongoro Forest Station means in Kikuyu 'the place of the bongo'; the bongo is a very rare and very beautiful antelope as big as a cow, bright red in colour with a dozen vertical white stripes, and with huge spiralled horns. It must have been common enough when the place first received its name, earlier in the century. Kiandongoro was, and possibly still is, as beautiful as the animal from which it takes its name. It is set deep in montane forest at an altitude of 7,000ft (2,150m) where the clear rivers cascade down deep ravines clothed in dense forest, but at that time the road to the Station from Nyeri must have been one of the worst in the world, especially difficult to negotiate in wet weather. A couple of hundred yards from the entrance to the Outspan the tarmac finished and troubles began. It was 12 miles (20km) of red earth with not a stone the whole way. Not only was it extremely slippery in wet weather but there was always an outward cant to the road, which had no semblance of a retaining wall, despite a drop of many hundreds of feet. If it rained, and rain was a common occurrence at Kiandongoro, only chains on the wheels would get you through. We always carried chains, spades, ropes, torches and everything else required for life on a lonely Forest Station, but fixing chains in the dark, in the rain, and in party clothes, is not a pastime to be recommended.

When circumstances were thus against us Gertrude Annie and I simply drove the car into the yard of the Outspan, had a drink, and waited for the duty driver at Kiandongoro to come and collect us, for he had orders to come for us if we had not arrived by a certain time. There was, of course, no telephone then. Maj Sherbrooke Walker ran the Outspan in those days, and was not surprised when, during the rainy season, he saw our car standing waiting to be collected the next day.

There was in those days, at the Outspan, a young Grevy zebra on the lawns. As far as I know it was never put to any specific use, but was just a pet. Probably it had been rescued after losing its mother. On the walls are a number of trophy heads of big game animals, and doubtless there are stories of interest behind each one, though these are now mostly lost in the mists of time. One, however, is the head of a water-buck bull killed in a fight with another water-buck, and there is a gilded plaque telling the story. Later the reader will learn how the Queen witnessed that fight. There is also a cast of a rainbow trout over 10lb (4.5kg) in weight. Fish of that size were by no means unknown in the Kenya of those days.

Although the Outspan Hotel is best known as the last home of Lord Baden-Powell, and the Nyeri Church as his last resting-place, and the road from the hotel to the churchyard is called Baden-Powell Road, it was also the last home of another famous man, and visitors who go to see the grave of the Chief Scout must pass within a few yards of the grave of this other. To my mind Jim Corbett was one of the greatest men who ever lived, though the world soon forgets, and, when mentioned, he is often confused with Jim Corbett ('Gentleman Jim') of boxing fame. I never knew Jim Corbett, for he died in 1955, the year before I was seconded back to Kenya, but I have paid him homage in his old home in India, which he left in the terrible days of Partition, and where no doubt his heart remained.

Jim Corbett, or to give him his full title Lt-Col Edward James Corbett, was born on 25 July 1875 at Gurney House in the foothills of the Himalayas, about 1,000ft (300m) above the hill station of Naini Tal, which itself lies at 7,400ft (2,250m). Still higher, and often covered in snow, towered the peak of Cheena. Jim Corbett's mother was married twice, her first husband being killed in the Indian Mutiny. Of that marriage there were four children, and of the second six sons and three daughters, a total of thirteen.

It was customary for middle-class Europeans of those days to live in the hills during the summer and on the plains during the winter, and so the Corbett family acquired a winter residence at Kaladhungi about the year 1862. Kaladhungi is 15 miles (24km) from Naini Tal, and, in the days of Jim Corbett's youth, he would think nothing of walking those 15 miles (24km) and back in order to attend Council meetings, leaving Kaladhungi before dawn and returning well after dark.

I have never seen Naini Tal, though I have seen the magic name on signboards, for in 1977 I had the great good fortune to be a guest of the Government of India and was taken in this capacity to Corbett National Park, named after Jim Corbett soon after his death, and to Kaladhungi. I saw my first tiger, and sat on the verandah where Jim and his sister Maggie would have been sitting in the evenings when runners came in to announce the latest brutal killings by a man-eater. I wandered in the now neglected garden and saw the flowering bushes and the Dorothy Perkins roses, now cankered and neglected. And in my mind I could see the ghosts of the past—Jim, Maggie and that wonderful little dog Robin. The artifacts on the wall and the table, the hurricane lamps and the simple crockery showed they lived a primitive life without electricity. Jim died the year before my return to Kenya but I remember the advertisements in the papers asking for his personal effects to be returned to his old home, which was being turned into a museum.

In Corbett National Park I rode an elephant whose mahout, an old silver-haired gentleman, had hunted with Jim Corbett. He would describe in mime how Sahib had always killed his tigers with one shot, and his faithful old eyes would light up at the memory. Jim Corbett's hunting career started in the last century, when he was only a boy, and he was tracking down man-eaters at government request very soon after. He shot his last man-eater when he was sixty-three. Tigers had killed and eaten people in considerable numbers in India since the days of the sabre-toothed cats, and since the Siberian tigers left the lands of snow and ice to find better hunting in the subcontinent and become the subspecific species we find today. However it was an outbreak of plague coupled with heavy poaching of the tigers' natural food that caused the crisis of Corbett's time. It was not only tigers but also leopards that became such terrible man-eaters, and when leopards start man-eating they are infinitely more difficult to deal with, being not only nocturnal but expert tree-climbers. It is spine-tingling to read Corbett's account of how one leopard killed and ate no fewer than three hunters who sat up in a tree, one after another, with the sole intention of shooting it. And one tiger, and one leopard between them, over a number of years, killed and ate no fewer than 836 people. This was the official figure and ignored those injured, who, in a land without antiseptics, would die eventually. Claws tainted with rotting meat invariably cause blood-poisoning.

In reading the endless stories of people being killed and eaten one is amazed to learn that all were unarmed, and that rarely was there any resistance; and this from a people who have been famous in war all through the ages. It must be remembered that these people were deeply superstitious and religious, and that invariably they were convinced that the tiger or leopard was not an ordinary animal but the spirit of some departed person returned on earth to wreak vengeance for some wrong supposedly done to him or her, and so thought that resistance would be futile.

Jim Corbett wrote six books altogether, and his first, written when he was sixty-nine, *Maneaters of Kumaon,* was such a success that one impression alone, that of the American Book of the Month Club, was 250,000 copies. It was translated into fourteen European languages, eleven Indian languages, Afrikaans and Japanese.

When World War I broke out in 1914 Jim Corbett, who was then thirty-nine, was considered too old for active service. However by 1917 things were different, and he was taken on to recruit a labour force from the people of Kumaon. He served with them in France, and was given the rank of captain. After that he saw fighting in the Third Afghan War, a little-known campaign but no doubt big enough for those who were involved.

In World War II, by which time he was in his sixties, he again recruited a labour corps and had to teach troops the art of jungle fighting, and for this he was commissioned lieutenant-colonel. He had an attack of typhus that caused him to lose a lot of weight and almost finished his active career. Then he went to Burma and had an attack of malaria that almost killed him.

The year 1947 brought the Partition of India, and Jim and Maggie decided to leave. No doubt a lot of their friends left at that time but Maggie always maintained that it was because they were both getting old and that a parting would have to come soon and that neither could face the prospect of living alone in India, much as they both loved the country. For some years Jim Corbett had been in partnership with a friend and had run a coffee farm in Tanganyika (now Tanzania). For three months every year he had left India to work there, and had built for himself a house, but it would seem the farm was sold, for there is no further mention of it. Another reason why Jim Corbett chose Kenya, and Nyeri in particular, to set up home rather than Tanzania was the fact that his nephew, Gen Tom Corbett, was already farming there; the latter's name quite often appears in the Treetops register as hunter-escort.

Jim Corbett and his sister Maggie lived in the cottage 'Paxtu', empty since the death of Lord Baden-Powell, until a few days before his death in Mount Kenya Cottage Hospital, a pleasant small place perched a few hundred yards higher up the Aberdares than the Outspan Hotel. He died quietly in his sleep only three months short of his eightieth birthday. Maggie lived on at the Outspan for some years. It has been said that behind every great man there is a great but unsung woman. This was certainly true of Jim Corbett. He was unquestionably a great writer and a fearless hunter, but it is also true that Maggie, with her keen memory for details of long past events and her own flair for writing, made her contribution. She is buried in the same grave as her brother, to the marble headstone of which were added simply the words 'and of his sister Maggie'.

In reading the books of Jim Corbett I always marvel at how he not only could spend all night sitting in a tree but could apparently sleep there with a certain degree of comfort. I only tried to spend such a night once, and I certainly didn't sleep much. It was in 1955, the year that Jim died. I had read none of his books and did not appreciate at that time what a great man he was. At that time I was a Forester in Mortimer Forest, near Ludlow in England, and fallow deer were nightly raiding the wheat of a farmer whose land the forest bordered. There was a solitary oak-tree in the middle of this wheat and my plan was to spend the night hidden there to be ready for the dawn. There were plenty of big branches, and I suppose Jim Corbett would have been as comfortable as the baboons at Treetops, but I didn't possess the callouses on the buttocks they have, and it was bitterly cold, though only late summer. I doubt if I did more than drowse and I was certainly glad when the dawn came. There was a solitary stag but he was out of range so eventually I clambered down and skirted the field on my way home. Apparently the stag decided to leave the field about the same time, and I met him on the path in the woods leading to my cottage and took him clean with one of the best rifle shots I had taken up to that time. Ever since I have wondered whether I would have got him just the same had I slept comfortably in bed and not tried to spend a night in a tree.

Other notables who have been to the Outspan or Treetops have included Tsar Ferdinand of Bulgaria and his niece, the Duke and Duchess of Gloucester, Mr and Mrs Neville Chamberlain, Queen Elizabeth the Queen Mother and Princess Anne, Earl Mountbatten and his daughter Lady Brabourne, Emperor Haile Selassie of Ethiopia, Willi Brandt of Germany and the head of state of almost every African country.

Humbler men and women have also played their part however. There is a Mrs Kay Willson, an old lady who still lives alone on a coffee farm at Kiganjo. She has supplied fruit and flowers to the Outspan and was once caretaker of State Lodge, Sagana. Kay, whose husband was an officer in the Indian Army, came out to Kenya in the retreat from Burma, and saw the atrocities of the Japanese. She lived through the worst of the Mau Mau. There were thugs who thought it was acceptable to raid the home of a lonely widow living on a coffee farm. At first they got away with it, stealing treasured possessions. One night they came in strength and bashed the door down with rocks. It happened, however, to be a night when her son was home for a few days and he greeted them with both barrels of a shotgun, killing one outright and wounding another. The wounded one was foolish enough to go to a hospital, where the police caught him; he is still in prison. Kay still lives alone.

Very little has been published concerning those earliest days of the Outspan Hotel, and I suppose that was because it was so little known to the outside world, but on 9 September 1930 an article by Lady Bettie concerning the excitements of running an up-country hotel in an undeveloped country like Kenya appeared in the British *Daily Mail.* She described how she and her husband would periodically take in people who were on a hunting safari. They would arrive in brand-new lorries filled with brand-new tentage and camping equipment and driven by hunters who looked as if they had just stepped off a Hollywood film set. A month later, or maybe three months later, they would return in vehicles battered and dusty, tents bleached and torn, but invariably with piles of skins, ivory tusks sticking out of corners, and wicked-looking buffalo and rhino heads protruding. Their faces would be brick-red from too much sun—but they would be happy.

She tells another story about how one evening a man came to the hotel and apologetically asked for a room in which to put a couple of lions. On being told that he could have room number 4 for himself and put his lions in room number 22 (number 22 had been slow about paying his bill) he replied that this would not do as he needed to share a room with his lions. He then went to his car and pulled out two snarling cubs about the size of dogs, explaining as he did so that he had shot the mother (in those days lions were vermin, to be shot on sight or even poisoned) and then discovered the cubs in the grass. With the aid of his African servant he had caught them up and bundled them into the car. He put them into the bathroom, occupied the adjacent bedroom, and fed them with a jug of milk every four hours. Next morning he paid his bill, installed the servant and the cubs in the back of the car, and left. Lady Bettie had not asked him where he was going, and he had volunteered no information.

Another story, which must be of the same era but is undated, can be read in the Outspan scrapbook. It is written in scrawling ink and there is no name attached. It concerns the night Denys Finch Hatton arrived at the hotel soaked to the skin, together with two African servants in a like condition.

Denys Finch Hatton will always be associated with *Out of Africa,* the classic book by Karen Blixen, or Baroness Karen Blixen-Finecke to give her her correct title, who had a coffee farm below the Ngong Hills not far out of Nairobi, and who also wrote under the pen name Isak Dinesen. In more recent years, authors, journalists and scriptwriters have portrayed Denys Finch Hatton as her lover. This, however, has been seen by many as a misrepresentation of facts, for though the friendship is known to have

The car of Denys Finch Hatton is pulled out of the Chania River after he and his servants had swum to safety. *(Block Hotel Archives)*

been a deep one, there is no proof that it was other than platonic.

Denys Finch Hatton's car had skidded on the Chania bridge outside Nyeri, and had fallen into the flooded river. It settled on the river-bed with its roof on the bottom and the wheels just above the level of the swirling water. Denys and the two Africans in the car were in imminent danger of drowning. He was a big and powerful man, and had made a name for himself in the field of athletics. He put his feet on the underside of the roof and his shoulders on the floor and heaved until the car and its roof parted. Then he pushed one of his two passengers out, whilst the other managed to extricate himself, and all three swam to the bank. Next morning, Eric Sherbrooke Walker went back with them to the scene and the car was salvaged and eventually started, so that they could motor back to Nairobi, but the roof had been washed away and was never found.

Soon after this, in 1931, Denys Finch Hatton was killed in a tragic 'plane crash, together with one of those two servants. He was flying his small aircraft from Voi to land on the airstrip on Karen Blixen's farm, and had just left Voi when something went wrong. He turned back but crashed before reaching Voi. He had confided to Karen Blixen that he wanted to be buried on the Ngong Hills, which was where they were picnicking at the time. Today there is a tall monument on the site, in what is now the Ngong Hills National Reserve and, beneath his name and the dates, are the words, 'He prayeth well who loveth well both man and bird and beast,' a quotation from Coleridge's *Ancient Mariner.* Lions often used to bask there in the morning sun. Denys Finch Hatton was a professional hunter of the old school, and must often have pitted his skills against similar big cats.

In the evenings of my days off-duty I invariably take my dog for a walk along the mile-long edge of the golf course, and I think about these people who helped make this country great and the place I am walking so beautiful: Karen Blixen who gave to Karen Estates its name and to the world some beautiful books; Sherbrooke Walker who built what must be one of the world's best-known hotels; Baden-Powell who created the Scout movement; and Jim Corbett who saved thousands of people from the jaws of the man-eaters and who gave his name to a National Park.

3
TREETOPS 1932–1952

Who built Treetops? We know that Sherbrooke Walker planned it, and we know that a Capt Sheldrick actually built it, but who had the brainwave in the first place? I have read just about every book, magazine article and press report written on the subject. They all have different versions and three books each give a different person—Eric, Lady Bettie and Sheldrick. All three are now dead, so let me tell a story, a story heard in the Treetops lounge some five years ago, and we will leave it at that.

A lady told me how she had been sitting on the sun-deck of a cruise liner, talking to another silver-haired old lady, and the subject turned to Treetops, which my informant hoped to visit one day. The second silver-haired old lady suddenly turned to the first and said: 'I built Treetops.' It was all very puzzling to my informant and she was too shy to ask a total stranger what she meant. With great satisfaction I explained to her that she could have been talking to none other than Lady Bettie herself, a great honour I was denied.

We do know for certain that, in the years following the building of the Outspan, Sherbrooke Walker not only was short of money (and so would be interested in a money-making new venture) but often used to take notables for walks into the nearby forest to observe wild animals, and that often he found himself, and his client, uncomfortably close to them. One such client was HM the King of Bulgaria, who, in addition to being an ardent lover of wildlife, was a keen entomologist. When out in the forest with Walker one day he followed a butterfly into a thicket in which a rhino was taking his midday snooze. The result was that the King very nearly ended up on the horn of the rhino.

A neighbour of Walker's, Capt Sheldrick, called always by the name of 'Ugly' Sheldrick, which he apparently did not object to (if he did he was overruled by his friends), had a farm on the edge of the forest; and, in a huge fig-tree overlooking a watering-hole, he had built a simple platform and rustic ladder, from which, on moonlit nights, he watched the wild animals drinking. Sheldrick, who knew of Walker's love of wildlife, invited him to spend a night there. The importance of this night will emerge in due course.

Not until I talked to a Maj James Nicolson did I learn more about those far off days. Nicolson came out to Kenya as a twenty-year-old in 1927 to manage the farm belonging to his aunt, a Mrs Page, at Mweiga. It was adjacent to that of Sheldrick, which was managed by a man called Scott, and Nicolson and Scott very often went hunting together in the area where Treetops now stands, to obtain meat for the community. One must remember that in 1927 there was no butcher's shops as such near, and, in the absence of a suitable animal on the farm to slaughter, one had to hunt for meat. Another neighbour, a Mr Wickham, had been killed by an elephant the previous year. Apparently his old rifle needed a tap on the breach after firing, and he carried a simple tool in his pocket to effect this. The elephant did not wait for the tap and the necessary reloading.

In 1930 Scott built a simple platform in the fig-tree, and it could well be that the idea behind it was to shoot animals for meat with less trouble. However, Sheldrick was soon using it on moonlit nights for game watching. Nicolson himself spent a night on that platform and he told me he was almost too cold and stiff next morning to climb down again.

In the autumn of 1930 Nicolson got the gold-rush fever, and went to Kakamega, in Western Kenya, where gold had just been discovered. Though he was there until the outbreak of World War II he never made much money prospecting. Very few settlers did, for the seams either ran out or went too deep. I was running Kakamega Forest in 1957 and my Land-rover fell into an old prospecting pit and was badly damaged, though I was not injured. We were planting Allosi Glade. One day when fishing the Yala River I came upon a gang illegally panning for gold. They promptly fled, leaving all their shovels, sieves and other equipment behind.

By the time Nicolson returned from the war, Treetops had been built, and when he asked if he could spend a night there the answer was yes, if he paid £5. This sum was at that time a large amount of money but to the general public the charge was £10, gaining Treetops the reputation of being the most expensive hotel in the world. Scott, it seems, left Kenya to run his mother's hairdressing salon in London, where he eventually died. What a far cry from his pioneer days of 1926 running a farm at Mweiga, and having sometimes to shoot his dinner in the forest or starve!

The morning after that night spent on the platform in the fig-tree the Sherbrooke Walkers talked it over. Eric wanted to show clients wild animals—or butterflies—without losing them on the horns of a rhino. Lady Bettie wanted a tree-house, a Wendy house like one she had played in as a child. Both of them wanted to make more money than the Outspan was making. And so between them the idea of Treetops was born, and Sheldrick was commissioned to build it.

On whose land was Treetops built? Again the published sources provide three different answers: Crown Land (half of Kenya was Crown Land at that time, owned by the Government and under the jurisdiction of the local District Commissioner); land belonging to the Forest Department (which was still in the process of being born); and the farm of Sheldrick. Months of research revealed finally that the now world-famous fig-tree was on gazetted Forest Department land, and that the gazettement was by Proclamation No 44 of 30 April 1932. A photostat copy of a map showing Boundary Plan No 175/13, to the scale 1:62,500, shows the Treetops pool as being nearly ½ mile (800m) inside the forest.

It was also revealed that Walker paid to the Forest Department a monthly rental of 20 shillings for the use of the tree, and that this concession was subject to cancellation at twenty-four hours' notice.

In pondering these things it must not be forgotten that the Kenya of 1932 was vastly different from the Kenya of today. The popular phrase 'miles and miles of bloody Africa' had meaning. It referred to an Africa hardly touched by the foot of man, where it was still possible to discover animals, birds and places unknown to the Western world. Treetops was opened to the public on 6 November 1932, but there is no record of just when the the first nail had been hammered into the tree. It could have been before that April gazettement, in which case the land was legally Crown. Again, the boundaries of farms were notoriously vague in those days, causing endless arguments, and it could well be that Sheldrick really thought he was still within the boundaries of his land when he put up the tree platform. Ted Honoré, who eventually became the Chief Conservator of the Forest Department, was posted to the Nyeri area as Divisional Forest Officer in 1932. He assures me that the forest boundaries had been fixed on the ground long before he arrived. Gazettements were certainly not carried out in a hurry in the Kenya of those days.

The first guest to spend the night at Treetops, that of 6 November 1932, was the man who physically built it, Capt 'Ugly' Sheldrick.

That well-built first Treetops had room for only two guests, and one of the Walkers had to do the necessary cooking, washing-up and bed-mak-

The Treetops built in 1932 was little more than a platform with rustic guard rails. (*Joan Davies*)

ing. The project grew and grew until, when the Queen came as a princess twenty years later it could accommodate eight, plus the African cook and his *mtoto* in a 'cubby-hole' beside the stove.

The first comprehensive picture of what a night spent at Treetops was really like comes from the pen of Mr R. O. Pearse. He and his wife spent the night of 2 June 1933 in Treetops and he wrote about it in a book called *Empty Highways*. He had just driven up to Kenya by car from Natal—quite an experience in itself. His book consists of twelve letters, from the places in Africa he considered the most interesting, and letter No 8 is headed 'The top of a tree, Mt. Kenya Forests, Kenya'. The Pearses had been conducted up to Treetops by Capt Sheldrick, but once there he had left them to take care of themselves. Treetops of course is not in the Mount Kenya forests but one must remember that there was no hard-and-fast line then between the two forest masses, and trees of one kind or another were almost everywhere. One must remember also that, though Treetops had been open for just over six months, its facilities were available only on nights when the moon was full.

Pearse recalls what a strange and eerie experience it was being left alone at dusk, but that his wife Edith had assured Sheldrick that she felt quite safe, and had forgotten her earlier terrors at the thought of being left alone. They had had quite an experience meeting an elephant in the forest even before they arrived. He says they saw a number of animals before dark, even though the pool was quite dry. Normally June is a month of heavy rains in Kenya, so 1933 must have been a drought year. Later a pump was to be installed, taking water from a very small river, the Muringato, some 3 miles (5km) away. Water, or rather the lack of it, has been a problem at Treetops from the beginning. Photographs show that the early water-hole was more in the nature of a swamp than a pool, and that it only became open water when an increasing number of animals ate the rushes.

When it became dark the Pearses went inside and cooked their evening meal. Light would be provided by a kerosene pressure lamp, or possibly just a hurricane lamp. Cooking would be done on an iron stove fired by wood. Apparently both elephants and rhinos arrived. Pearse vividly describes some of the night sounds and laments the fact that he did not even have a torch. It must be remembered that in 1933 animals were indeed frightened of a light, whether it was a torch or the headlights of a car, for it was invariably followed by a bullet. A lot of the weird noises would be made by the tree hyrax. For those who are not familiar with this rabbit-sized animal, the coney of the Bible and the nearest living relative of the elephant, it should be explained that the noises made by the hyrax, whether it be the tree or the rock species, are terrifying. The tree hyrax lives in hollow trees, which greatly magnify the sound; the noise consists of impressive shrieks rising to a crescendo and finally subsiding into a banshee wail, only to start all over again.

Pearse relates that, back at the Outspan next day, Walker described to him how it was when Treetops was under construction. Every day, apparently, a rhino would charge the builder, and each time it charged he put up his price a little.

There is no further description of a night spent at Treetops until it had become much more widely known, and hunters, to be followed later by hostesses, were a regular feature. The cost per night was set at £10, but nobody appears to have grumbled. Walker introduced his famous 'No animals no paying' scheme, whereby if no giant beasts were sighted the client did not pay. In those days the buffalo herds were still recovering from the awful rinderpest outbreak at the end of the last century and on many days none was seen. Today I have counted over 300 coming in to drink at dawn, a long, endless black line emerging from the forest and then disappearing back into it.

45

What kind of tree was Treetops built in? In all the many thousands of words written there is no indication of the species of fig-tree in which the 1932 Treetops was built. Usually the tree is simply identified as a fig-tree; sometimes it is described as a Migumu tree, a Kikuyu name for fig; sometimes the word *ficus* is used, the Latin name for all figs.

There are thirty-four species of fig-tree reported in Kenya, and all books stress that, because the figs become mouldy in the press due to latex exuding when cut, collecting has not been thorough and more species could yet be discovered. A study of photographs, and of other fig-trees in the vicinity, shows that the Treetops fig-tree was undoubtedly *Ficus natalensis*, the Bark Cloth Fig.

Fig-trees are common throughout Kenya, partly because of the ease with which they coppice, and partly because they are useless as firewood. They are tolerated in cultivated areas because they have the rare property of conserving moisture in the soil, and increase its fertility. Plants can grow in their shade. Above all the Wakikuyu hold the fig-tree in reverence, as a haunt of spirits, and their religious and circumcision ceremonies are always held in its shade. Outside every village will be seen a small copse dominated by one or more of these trees. So strong is this reverence for the fig-tree that one must be very careful to avoid cutting down such a tree.

Fig-trees will grow easily from cuttings and from stakes, and in the wild the majority start life as an epiphyte, slowly strangling the host tree with their all-embracing branches. After the death they become self-supporting, and often no trace of the host can be seen. Seeds are usually dropped by monkeys or by birds into a root crevice where they quickly germinate.

The Bark Cloth Fig is particularly common in the mountain forests but also occurs elsewhere. In Uganda it is still used as cloth, being hammered on stones until the bark ór bast acquires the desired cloth-like texture. The fruit is not big enough to attract humans but is much appreciated by monkeys and hornbills. There is a huge fig-tree of this species halfway down the river walk from the Outspan Hotel to the Chania River. The path actually goes through the centre of the tree, and the aerial roots hang down like a curtain. There is another very fine specimen halfway between Treetops and another game-viewing lodge—the Ark. This is Kimathi's fig-tree, and was used extensively by both Mau Mau and the security forces for posting letters, between two huge entwining branches, when Dedan Kimathi was a Mau Mau leader and the British were trying to persuade him to surrender. A third stands beside the bridge over the Chania, and would doubtless have been there when Denys Finch Hatton ditched his car in the river more than half a century ago.

Reading through the early log-books kept at Treetops it is interesting to note the birds and animals using the fig-tree as their home, and that the fact that there were humans living in the tree does not appear to have worried them. A hammerkop nested in the tree regularly. This big brown frog-eating bird with a hammer of feathers on the head makes a huge domed nest of grass, which grows year by year, sometimes until it would fill a hay-cart. There is always a hole in the side of the nest, through which the young glide into water; so the hammerkop's presence is proof as to Treetops' vicinity to the pool. A hornbill, presumably the black-and-white casqued, nested regularly in a hole in the fig-tree. Only in recent years has it been discovered that the male walls up the female in the hole and feeds her throughout both incubation and the nestling stage. Yet here we have evidence that tourists lived within a few feet of such birds fifty years ago and presumably photographed the very act. Bush-babies and genets were resident throughout the twenty years from 1932 to 1952 and a saucer of milk would be put down for them. By day the marvellously quick little tree squirrels darted about the branches. There are no records of tree hyrax, but the forest would echo every night to their unearthly screams. They love old, half-dead hollow trees. Even today we can hear them, though not very near, and only the other day one came into the huge pear-

The Treetops pool in 1932, taken by an unknown photographer and showing it as a swamp. Captioned in the Block Hotels Archives album as 'first elephant seen at Treetops'

wood tree growing through the centre of Treetops and crouched on the topmost branch until dark. I am sure it was driven into the tree by a predator, probably a mongoose.

Baboons feature regularly in the earliest photographs of Treetops, though not in the numbers in which we find them today, for they have proliferated as more and more food has become available. Baboons are the only animals we do not even try to count today. We work on the assumption that Treetops was built for the baboons, just as *they* do, yet, when the maize is ripening in the nearby lands they can absent themselves for a few days, walking past the building soon after dawn and marching like an army, adults in the front, children playing in the centre, and more adults bringing up the rear. It is indeed an army, for a few are always shot when raiding the maize, yet it makes no difference; the others always return again the next day. In the evening we see them marching back to the roosting trees with full bellies.

An animal virtually absent today is the Cape hunting dog, yet they were recorded regularly in those early days; indeed they were on the list of animals it was possible to see as late as 1960. Hunting dogs would move from the plains into the forests whenever there was a shortage of game or when they fancied a change. They are full of curiosity, and once, deep in the forests of Mount Kenya, I was suddenly surrounded by them, all standing on their hindlegs to see me better over the bushes. National Park rangers still record the occasional meeting with hunting dogs on the Aberdares during their patrols, but the elimination of this creature started when the plains were cultivated, and virtually ended when a deep ditch was dug for 23 miles (37km) around the Park boundary, especially when it was topped with an electric fence.

It would be wrong to think of Treetops as being deep within the forest, even in 1932, for whistling thorn trees are not far away, and these are trees of the dry country. A further proof is that a solitary impala hung around Treetops for a month recently, and that Jim Corbett's little book *Treetops* depicts impala at the pool.

Animal life has changed dramatically at Treetops since 1932; this will be discussed in greater detail in a later chapter, 'Retreat of the Forest'.

(*Opposite*) The modern Treetops Hotel seen across the pool, note the tree growing up through the middle of the hotel
(*Overleaf above*) Rhinoceros fighting near Treetops, now an endangered species (*Photo by Fred M. Doner*) (*Overleaf below*) A bongo with her young (*Photo by J. V. Spalding*)

What was the Treetops pool like originally? All over the Aberdares are what are known as 'ridge pools' and the pools at Treetops and the Ark are classic examples. Ridges are always favourite animal gathering places, for they are vantage points from which to look down upon enemies from afar, and to smell them on rising air currents. It must be remembered that Man has been the greatest of all predators since he first started to use primitive weapons, and to use his brain deliberately to plan, more than 50,000 years ago. The Aberdares themselves are much older than that, and it is reasonable to suppose they were vegetated, and populated by animals, about that time and that roving bands of men ventured there, though they found it too cold for habitation.

Those early animal gatherings merely created hollows by the removal of earth on the feet, but these soon filled with rainwater, more mud was created, and the rate of removal accelerated as wallowing also took place. Soon a definite pool was formed, and it attracted more and more animals, especially in dry weather, and an increasing deposit of urine and dung added minerals, salts and trace elements to the soil. In montane rain-forests of the type found in the Aberdares there is a distinct shortage of these, due partly to the leaching caused by a high rainfall but also to a fast run-off on the steep slopes. This is illustrated by the alacrity with which bull buffaloes proceed to the place where rhino have urinated and lick the soil, and the speed with which animals converge upon an area that has been salted. Unscrupulous hunters have been known to salt an area in the forest, then shoot over it, especially for bongo. Similarly, when cattle *bomas* are changed and the old hedges burned, impala, zebra and giraffe quickly congregate on the old sites.

Perhaps the most bizarre illustration is to watch a snoozing buffalo at night and see a hyena belly-crawl up to him and lick around the buffalo's anus, where a considerable amount of dung always dries. Sometimes the buffalo will tolerate this action for a while before levering himself up and chasing the hyena away.

Another factor which favoured the development of the Treetops pool was that it lay directly in the path of an old migration trail linking Mount Kenya and the Aberdares, used mostly by elephants. Migrating animals in Kenya have never been known to carve a path through solid rock in the

(*Previous page*) A baboon cleaning her young
(*Opposite*) The author escorting HM The Queen around the old Treetops site during her nostalgic return visit in 1983 (*Photo by Tim Graham*)

way bison did when they migrated from the Rockies to the Prairies every year; nevertheless I have seen places where the trail was quite deep.

Where was the salt-lick in 1932? I doubt that there was ever a natural salt-lick at Treetops, 'In spite of the talk by learned people about cobalt and suchlike. In 1960, when I was the Forester at Kiandongoro, I was asked to participate in a research project on that part of the Aberdares under my control. My twenty Forest Guards were deployed every day with little bags to places where they knew wild animals congregated, with instructions to fill the bags with soil. These were then sent to Nairobi to be analysed. The results were always the same—no salts other than those associated with urine and dung.

It should be mentioned here that those great wanderers, the elephants, would visit any road-building project on the Aberdares and, within days, dig up the exposed earth in their search for minerals. Also, when trees fell down during a storm, or there was a landslide, they would be quickly there.

When Treetops was first built it was, as explained earlier, in the Forest Reserve and there were no restrictions whatever to attracting animals to the place. In addition to salt it was quite possible to put down cabbages, sugar-cane and anything else that came to mind. This was of course done. The land did get a rest during both World War II and the latter part of the Kenya Emergency, but the retreat of the forest due to a combination of many factors unquestionably commenced in 1932 and has continued to this day.

Today the National Park authority is adamant that salt, plain sodium chloride, is the only substance permissible for attracting animals, and this ruling has been strictly followed since 1950. Nevertheless the retreat of the forest at Treetops may cause them to change their views. My own conclusion is that salt should be put down only by the Parks themselves and that the practice should cease in a particular area as soon as an environmentalist makes this recommendation.

This chapter, covering the first twenty years of Treetops, must of necessity sometimes depart from the chronological sequence in its description of what it was like. Records are few, memories are dim, and so many of the people who took part are no longer with us. In the earliest days there was a crow's-nest on the very highest branch, reached only along a rickety plank-type ladder, and guests took turns to sit there. There was an Elsan chemical toilet on another distant branch, again reached by a rickety ladder. Baggage was hoisted aloft by a winch, and guests themselves climbed a very steep ladder with a platform halfway, and this was pulled up after the last person was safely aboard. In later years all these features were to be abolished on the grounds of the fire hazard.

Folding camp-beds, or metal cots, were an obvious means of econo-mising space, as were blankets hung as 'partitions' and walls of papyrus stems bound tightly together. All the major branches of the tree were allowed to grow through the building, padded with felt in places where they might injure bald heads. Tables and chairs were of the camping type, and there was even a bar, for the settler of 1932 must never miss his sun-downer, or the whisky that kept away the malaria. Nobody handled such a mundane thing as money; guests just signed in the book for their drinks and poured their own. Hot-water bottles were once put in the beds, tea was brought to the rooms, and a cuckoo-clock hung on the wall, its alien call announcing every half-hour of the day and night.

All water, whether for cooking, drinking or the 'splashing' which sub-stituted for a wash in the safari bowls, had to be carried on the heads of porters. Every gallon of petrol, every pound of ghee or cooking fat, that entered the country did so in a 4gal (18l) *debe* and so these ubiquitous vessels became the universal container used for carrying. (And when the *debes* began to leak and were no longer useful as carriers they were flattened and used as roofing tiles on huts and *dukas* (Asian shops) from Mombasa to Nairobi, to the Red Sea coast. The wooden boxes in which the *debes* arrived, arranged side by side, were never wasted, but were used for making furniture, or piled one on top of the other as shelves.) The porters, who wore little more than a blanket, would put a ring of woven grass upon their heads on which to rest the heavier loads. Their feet would be bare, or at best they would wear sandals of animal hide or, if sophisticated, cut from old car tyres. They would carry a *panga* (machete), tied to the waist if their hands were not free, for in the Africa of 1932 it was not safe to walk about without one.

Today, in a Kenya which caters for 300,000 tourists a year and is talking about an annual million in the future, the regulations in force at Treetops between 1932 and 1952 appear incredible. Perhaps the only place in the world which still makes anything like the same stipulations is Tiger Tops in Nepal. Dress had to be safari-type, and any suggestion of red would have resulted in the wearer being left behind. Silence had to be total, and any loitering on the forest path in order to take photographs from behind, a much favoured ploy today, resulted in a severe reprimand. Smoking was taboo, either in or out of doors. Baggage all had to be carried by the porters, for such things were a hindrance to quick movement up ladders installed along the route. The order 'Up ladders' meant just that, and no delaying to take photos. The ability to walk sturdily, for the most part up a particularly

Treetops in the mid-thirties shows a slight improvement

steep hill, was taken for granted. During inclement weather guests were expected to be well shod, but to change into slippers the moment they were 'up the tree'.

Upon arrival at the end of the long valley, the point where vehicles could go no further, everybody climbed out of the safari cars, usually box-body Ford Tens with wire-mesh sides and a canvas curtain which could be rolled down to keep away a little of the dust. Then they listened to the 'White Hunter'—a term long since abolished in Kenya—and he would load his heavy rifle, always a double in those days. He would *not* smile, and he would tell them just what they could and could not do. There was a rack of stout walking sticks ready to be handed out. It consisted of a trophy-sized water-buck skull resting on a rustic stand with the horns acting as a cradle. The tourists needed those stout walking sticks to help them up the steep hill. Leading them would be the hunter with his loaded rifle at the ready, followed by the women, then the men, then a few *askaris* carrying spears, and finally the porters with their head loads of baggage, food and *debes* full of water. Every few yards, wherever there were suitable trees, rough ladders were nailed to tree-trunks. Sometimes, if the trees were big enough, the ladder would be wide enough for three or four people to climb up side by side.

Mention of the 'chop boxes' that carried the food for the night's supper always reminds me of my 1956 return to Kenya. 'Suez' occurred whilst we were on our way and all our possessions were caught at sea and rerouted around the Cape instead of through the Canal. We were in quite a predicament until a Forester friend said: 'Put in a claim for safari equipment and mark it urgent.' Amongst the pots and pans that duly arrived was a chop box, a stout wooden box with a lid, and capable of holding the 40lb (18kg) that made up the standard porter's load.

The earliest Treetops—the two-guests-only structure—had a manhole over the first landing, the idea being to stop any inquisitive leopard following the last visitor aboard. This was not as remote a possibility as one might think. There are always a few wild animals infinitely more bold and more capable than the average. Secret Valley, constructed some years later on Mount Kenya, and again in a Forest Reserve, had the speciality of feeding leopards from three feeding platforms just 18ft (5.5m) from the balcony, and tourists were told this so that they could adjust their cameras. At 3am one morning a tourist came out of his bedroom to be confronted by a leopard on the verandah. They had to change their ideas about the 18ft (5.5m). Samburu Lodge fed crocodiles for years on the far side of a 3ft (90cm) wall. The area was called the Crocodile Bar, and was very popular. That wall is now a foot higher, for one night an extra big croc just flipped over it.

The manhole at Treetops was abolished eventually because one fat visitor got stuck in it. Somebody pulled from above, and somebody pushed from below, but it was all in vain. Then someone had the idea of opening up the bar and bringing down a strong liqueur. After suitable rounds the super effort was made and the man was freed.

There must have been many strange incidents at Treetops that have remained unrecorded, and it is a great pity; but two at least have been documented. In such surroundings spirits run high, and it is not surprising that bets and dares have been made. One recorded incident concerned the only professional hunter of the fair sex, the other a lady of unquestionable beauty. The professional lady hunter took out clients, and it is said she was in great demand by those who wished to obtain good trophies but did not have any particular leanings towards ladies as such. She was, it was said, a lady of exceptional manly behaviour. Her ambition in life, apparently, was to fix a stamp on an elephant's bottom at Treetops. To do this she needed plenty of sturdy helpers, a good thick rope and a co-operative elephant standing in just the right spot beneath the building. All of these prerequisites were eventually fulfilled, and overboard she went, securely

The cosy bar of early Treetops. Even in 1969 soft drinks could be accounted for in this way until the barman came on duty in the evening. (*G. A. Mason Smith, senior hunter at Treetops for many years*)

tied to the rope. Hilarity, however, ran at such a pitch that the stalwarts on the rope end let it slip through their hands and she landed fairly on the back of the startled elephant. Fortunately at this stage mirth turned to anxiety and she was hauled back before a tragedy could occur, and the madcap experiment was not repeated.

The other adventure was conceived by a lady of feminine beauty and build. She was determined to write her name on an elephant's bottom, using a piece of chalk tied to the tip of a billiard cue. The billiard cue, however, was not long enough to reach that part of the elephant standing so fortuitously below the building. So once again the rope was brought out and tied around the waist. Walker himself is reported as having carried out the job and, in his book *Treetops Hotel*, he laments the fact that his knowledge of the female anatomy was so poor that he got his centre of balance all wrong. Maybe she was overendowed in certain places, or maybe he *was* ignorant. Whatever the cause no sooner was she clear of the building than she turned upside down, and no amount of kicking would bring her the right way up. Eventually she had to be hauled back, the elephant having refused to wait.

There is, apparently, only one recorded case of a rhino causing a serious problem, though it was much more common in the early days than it is today. A party was halfway to Treetops when a truculent rhino appeared on the path, and the order went out, 'Up trees'. There was in the group, however, a young man who badly wanted a photograph of a charging rhino, and he thought this was his great opportunity. He stayed on the ground until the beast was really close, then attempted to climb up the tree. But he had left it too late and, in his haste, the camera slipped out of his hands and the strap went over the front horn of the beast. The rhino disappeared into the bushes festooned with the camera, the hunter vented his wrath on the unfortunate but disobedient guest, and the guest demanded his camera back. This the hunter flatly refused, and the guest was too frightened to venture into the bushes alone. And that, apparently, was the end of the matter, with the camera gone for ever.

One night a man of my own age came to Treetops, and told me the following story. During World War II he had served in Abyssinia, now Ethiopia, and when the campaign was over he had been sent on leave to a settler's farm, the arrangements having been made by the East African Women's League. Up to that point the story was exactly the same as mine. I had been sent 'West of Rift', but he had been sent 'East of Rift', to a farm not far from Treetops, but of course he had never heard of the latter at the time.

One day he was trying out his meagre knowledge of Swahili on a servant—English was virtually unknown to most Africans at that time—when the servant suddenly said: 'Would you like to see a funny little house up in a tree? I will take you into the forest and show you one if you will come with me.' Intrigued by this, and not really believing him, the soldier set off on a long walk into the forest. It was the heat of the day, when so many animals are lying down, and throughout that long walk they did not see a thing. They were lucky. At last they came to a huge fig-tree, though he did not know one tree from another, and in the branches was a strange house, with a steep ladder leading upwards, a house that was to become world-famous a decade later. The rooms were all locked, and they could only peep through the windows. During World War II there must have been very many nights when Treetops stood empty like that, regardless of the full moon, for Eric Sherbrooke Walker was away in the war too. Not until 1952 was the narrator of this story aware of what he had seen that day in the forests of Kenya, and from that moment he saved until he had enough money to come back.

4

A LODGE, A CHURCH,
A POLO MATCH AND A CLUB

In 1951 Sir Philip Mitchell was the Governor of Kenya Colony, and, when he heard that Princess Elizabeth and the Duke of Edinburgh were coming for a holiday he thought it would be a wonderful idea to give them a game-viewing lodge in one of the newly gazetted National Parks as a rather belated wedding present. Accordingly he sent for Col Mervyn Cowie, the Executive Officer of the Nairobi National Parks, and told him of his plans, asking him to choose a site, preparatory to building a lodge.

Cowie was delighted, and quickly set about the job, assisted by Ken Beaton, Warden of the National Park. The place they chose was on the southern promontary of the Ngong Hills, the traditional home of the Maasai tribe. The view from this site was indeed superb, and had been described by Gen Smuts as the most inspiring in Africa. The land was teeming with wild animals. At the turn of the century there had been elephants, though none had visited since 1926. He reported back to the Governor, the site was accepted and Cowie built a rough approach road and engaged the services of a good architect to prepare plans for this dream lodge.

It was at that stage the Governor announced that he had changed his mind and had chosen a site on Mount Kenya, a remote area at that time, and that all involved must meet him by the Sagana River, so that he could show them the place. Why the Governor changed his mind will never now be known but he must have had some reason other than the rather naive one given of too many burrs in the bushes. The new site had no animals visible as they were on the plains; the forest was both difficult to walk in and dangerous; there was no view of the mountain; and the access road would be long and would therefore be expensive to build. Only on the grounds of fishing could the area be said to be unique, but Britain itself has some of the finest fishing in the world available to royalty. The Governor would not rescind his decision, and Cowie asked leave to withdraw from all responsibility in the project.

With the benefit of hindsight it is now possible to say that Sagana is a better site. Recently I flew over the Ngong Hills and was appalled to see how the city of Nairobi has eaten up those 20 miles (32km); what was once a beautiful vista of Africa is now suburbia.

Before leaving the subject of the Ngong Hills site for that of the first lodge it should be mentioned that only at the last minute was the Nairobi National Park included in the royal party's itinerary for their five-day holiday. There were rumours that captured lions were put on view, but that of course was rubbish. What actually happened was that lions were followed, but only at the last moment was a kill found in a deep ravine. It was pulled out onto open ground and the Princess was extremely lucky to get the good photographs she did.

The building of Sagana Royal Lodge then became the responsibility of the Ministry of Works (often called the PWD—Public Works Department), and was completed just in time for the royal visit. Up to window level the lodge was built of beautifully dressed stone cut by masons brought in from Nairobi; above were double-faced timber off-cuts, and then a cedar shingle roof. The walls were lined with boards of cedar and podo, giving a charming two-shaded effect. A Col Sharp ('Sharpie') from Thomson's Falls was employed to do the landscape gardening, and a wonderful job he is recorded as having made of it. The lawns sloped down to the Sagana River.

Treetops during a severe drought soon after being built. Note lack of leaves, water and grass. (*Block Hotel Archives*)

The Duke's bedroom is reported to have been in naval style, with large drawers under the bed. I am indebted to Mrs Beverley of Nairobi for information regarding the furniture. She tells me that it was made by a Mr George Dennis, a famous cabinetmaker who was working with the Ministry of Works at that time. The beauty of the furniture is remembered by John Cobby after more than thirty-two years. All reports are unanimous that a eucalyptus (Australian gum) plantation gave an adverse impression on arrival but that the scene changed dramatically as one proceeded up the drive.

An amusing account of the arrival of the Princess and the Duke in February 1952 comes from the pen of Mrs Kate Challis, whose father, Gen Beynon, was a soldier settler in the Mweiga area in 1919. She now lives at Karen, near Nairobi. She recalls that the East African Women's League was asked to arrange the flowers, and that four of the members, Patience Windley, wife of the Provincial Commissioner Sylvia Richardson, Kim Doig and herself went by car to Sagana with a choice selection of flowers provided by farmers' wives from miles around. It was a much bigger job than they had anticipated, and they had quickly to gather up the debris off the floor and escape out of the back door as the Princess entered by the front. They hid, and after the royal party had left returned and finished off the job, never dreaming that it would next be seen by a queen, following the momentous events described in the next chapter.

That visit was strictly private, and Kate Challis relates that one of the press came up to her and asked her price for smuggling him up in the back of her car. Her reply, apparently, was not polite. Because of the private nature of the stay at Sagana Royal Lodge little is known about it, and photographs are rare. The Duke planted a podocarpus tree in the grounds, and Kay Willson, who was caretaking for a time, tells me it developed a bark disease which she reported and which was finally cured.

A lovely story comes from the police of those days. In a pool of the Sagana River, at the bottom of the lawn, lived a very big trout which was fed every evening, and the Princess was given a plate of food to offer it. After the visit of the royal party the Police took over the lodge because of Mau Mau. Eventually a young officer was posted there who was a very keen fisherman, and unfortunately he very soon caught the mammoth trout. When the police headquarters in Nairobi heard about it they were furious, and posted him to an arid area near the coast, with the comment that it would be hard for him to find any trout there.

Whilst staying at the Royal Lodge the Princess and the Duke went trout fishing twice. During the first evening they caught a half-dozen of the ½lb

(225g) and ¾lb (340g) class. During the second trip they caught the same number but the fish were rather smaller and so were returned. They also went horse-riding before breakfast on the 1,000 acre (400ha) ranch of the Windleys. Considering they were only five days in the country their stay was well filled with the pleasures of country life.

When independence came to Kenya, eleven years later, the Princess, then Queen, gave Sagana Royal Lodge to the new republic. Jomo Kenyatta, the country's first president, renamed it Sagana State Lodge, and used it as his own private residence whenever he was touring in that part of the country. He also had a residence at Nakuru. When President Moi, who was elected president upon the death of Kenyatta, visited England on a state visit in 1979, he invited Queen Elizabeth back to Kenya, an invitation she was unable to take up for four years. President Moi was fully aware of the necessity of a refuge from the blaze of publicity a state visit always attracts. He was also aware of the very special place the lodge must always have in the heart of the Queen because it was the place where she was informed of her father's death in 1952. He ordered that Sagana Lodge be made ready for her. It is recorded that, though the building had changed much, she remembered the grounds.

The British monarch is head of the Church as well as head of state. It was, therefore, but natural that the planners of Princess Elizabeth's five-day 1952 holiday in Kenya should include a church service, for she was heir to the throne. Amongst her future subjects were settlers who had carved out their farms from the wilderness, and up and down the country were the churches they had built for themselves on a voluntary basis. St Philip's was chosen, a small church built only two years previously by the tiny community of farmers around Naro Moru. These settlers provided most of the labour and the materials, yet the records show that St Philip's Church, on the Nyeri–Nanyuki road, cost 26,060 shillings 99 cents to build, a considerable amount of money at that time. Maj G. Baynes gave the land on which it was built and the foundation stone was laid on 24 July 1949. The church was consecrated the following year.

St Philip's stands on the banks of the Naro Moru River, a small clear trout-stream flowing off the nearby snows of Mount Kenya to the east. It is made of well-dressed local stone and has a cedar shingle roof through which the sunlight glitters, yet, according to Mr Ron Nelson, who showed me around, no rain ever comes through. Though still less than forty years old it has a mellowed look reminiscent of English churches very many years older.

The great day came for St Philip's Church when HRH Princess

Elizabeth attended divine service on 5 February 1952, the morning before going to Treetops. She subsequently allowed her coat of arms to be hung in the church, and the beautiful 25ft (7.5m) long blue carpet came from Westminster Abbey after her coronation on 3 May 1953. A Mrs Facey, wife of the Nyeri Road Engineer, made the coat of arms in silk from a picture supplied by Westminster Abbey. A tree was planted by Maj Baynes to commemorate the occasion, and is alive and healthy today, though considering it is thirty-two years old is not as big as one would expect. This, no doubt, is due to the stony nature of the ground. Why an exotic species, Brazilian rosewood (*Macherium tipu*) was chosen, when Kenya possesses so many very beautiful indigenous flowering trees, is hard to understand.

Mr Ron Nelson was with the police on crowd control that day, and so could not attend the service, but he says he saw over sixty people sitting on chairs outside. The congregation was apparently chosen from the regular members of the three churches of Nyeri, Naro Moru and Nanyuki. The Rev Gerald Knight was chaplain, and he took the service. Inside the church I found a prayer-book, and written inside in rather faded ink were the words: 'This prayer book was used by HRH The Duke of Edinburgh on 5.2.1952.'

As related in an earlier chapter, at the end of the Abyssinian campaign I obtained a long weekend leave and went to the home of Capt Pat Kinealy, whose farm at Naro Moru bordered that of Maj Baynes. It was called Wanki Wonki because when he lay abed at night and listened to the braying of zebras being chased by lions he reckoned the noise sounded just like those two words. Pat Kinealy was one of the first to farm in the area, at the end of World War I, and before he could even start to raise cattle he had to reduce the huge rhino population which dominated the whole area. Every door of his sprawling bungalow had a rhino horn for a stopper, and some of them were so big one did not need to stoop in order to move them. He had shot each one himself. In those days the African had no use whatsoever for rhino horn.

Kinealy Pat was also one of the unsung heroes of the war in Tanganyika (now Tanzania) where he helped chase the Germans out. He told me that his limp was caused by a burst of seven machine-gun bullets in the leg. One passed through his water-bottle, and before he lost consciousness he felt the liquid running and thought he had been shot through the bladder!

When on that visit to Pat Kinealy I fished the beautiful Naro Moru River. I must have travelled very close to where the church stands today, and where a Princess was to pray a decade later. She was there just twenty-four hours before she became Queen. Did the quiet solitude of that beautiful place and the unswerving loyalty of all those people who were to become her subjects help to consolidate the strength she was later to find to reign over an empire, later a commonwealth, constituting nearly half the peoples of the world?

A series of friendly polo matches was arranged for the afternoon of Monday 4 February 1952 by the settler members of the Nyeri Polo Club at their Mweiga ground, some 3 miles (5km) from Treetops. Knowing how keen a polo player the Duke was, and the Princess's interest in horses, the royal couple was invited to participate.

It was a gloriously sunny day, as February days usually are, and Mount Kenya could be seen clearly. The Duke played a total of eight chukkas, choosing a number of different ponies from the large number available in the long, thatched stables adjacent to the clubhouse. One of these was a fine, big-boned grey mare called Poppet, owned by Col Derick Richardson who farmed at Kiganjo. Another was called Corky. In the early afternoon it was still quite hot, and, after the second chukka, it was suggested that a break for drinks was justified, and the players retired to the clubhouse. As they climbed the steps one of them called out to the Duke: 'Can I order you a drink, Sir?' The answer came back quickly: 'Might be better if you ordered a hearse.' The royal couple were straight out from the depths of an English winter, and the Duke was playing against men who had spent many years in Kenya. The polo ground was virtually on the equator at an altitude of 7,000ft (2,150m).

The Duke enjoyed his drink and reportedly played much better afterwards. Sylvia Richardson remembers how excited the Princess was as she watched from the touchline, and the look of admiration in her eyes as the Duke galloped near. Between chukkas she was busy being presented to a long line of waiting residents. Sylvia also remembers how, at the end, when drinks were flowing and the gossip was general, some of the farmers wanted to smoke but dared not, for the Princess was, and still is, a non-smoker, and she remembers how difficult it was arranging for a request to be made, but how very gracious the Princess was in agreeing.

In his book *Treetops*, Jim Corbett relates that he and his sister Maggie both hated crowds, and how worried he was about the Princess's safety. The 'Emergency' had not yet been declared, and the name 'Mau Mau' had not yet been applied, but a number of murders had already taken place and acts of violence were common, but for obvious reasons the situation had been played down by the press. The forests of the Aberdares were not very far away, and a deep ravine made an easy approach for terrorists almost up to the polo ground. So Jim and Maggie went together in their car to the bottom of the ravine and stopped by a little wooden bridge, and searched in the soft sand for any traces of footprints. Although they never found any they stayed the rest of the afternoon there and so missed much of the play.

Today, virtually the whole of the valley is under cultivation. The bridge that Jim Corbett talked about has been replaced by concrete culverts, and the flow of water is so small that for most of the year it merely forms a swamp, only coming over the road during very heavy rains. In 1952 human activity at that bridge was slight; since then water has been pumped to irrigate the vastly increased planted areas of coffee, to supply a very much enlarged Treetops, a National Parks Headquarters and five camping sites.

During my research I found a number of older men among the Treetops staff who could remember the forest as it was more than thirty years ago, though most of them were then but children herding goats. They can remember elephants coming down to that bridge almost nightly to drink, and how one particular rhino used to chase them all until the Game Department finally came and shot it.

I never watched a game of polo myself until Eddie Fernandes, who farms on Mount Kenya and who has helped me so much with this book, invited me to a match being played on his huge ranch. Until then I thought the game had died out with Independence. How wrong I was, and how much I enjoyed watching it. I have always been interested in horses, and must be the only Forester who has habitually *ridden* around his forests in both Britain and Kenya. My first pony was bought at Hardknott Forest in the English Lake District. She was a Dales, a sturdy fell pony much used in Yorkshire, and was black with white socks and blaze. Her name was Sally, and she took me up mountainsides that were negotiable only on foot. I rode her 40 miles (64km) one weekend to meet a beautiful Arab stallion at Hawkshead. The resulting foal was a chestnut, and I called him Beau Brummel. I broke him and trained him myself. Beau Brummel was my pride and joy when I was posted to Ludlow, in Shropshire, two years later, in 1952. Ludlow is famous not only for its castle but for its fox-hunting and racing. I rode him all over my forest and, when the going was tough, I would dismount and he would follow me like a dog.

One afternoon, in my office, I bet my boss, Ike Adams, that I would beat him to the place where the men were working, with him in his Land-rover and me on Beau Brummel. The odds were not as long as they sound, for there were numerous gates that Beau Brummel could take in his stride, and the track in the forest was deeply rutted in places so that the Land-rover had to take care in negotiating them. Beau Brummel was running loose in an old plantation of spruce, but he always came at the gallop when called. I

A group of seven guests walk the narrow, steep, densely forested path of Treetops Hill. The habit of issuing stout sticks now appears to have been abandoned. *(Keystone Press Agency Ltd)*

had no time to be bothered with tack and rode him bareback, his mane and long tail flying, and won with ease, much to the surprise of my boss.

Soon after my secondment to Kenya in 1956 I was given a huge grey mare by a Forester who had just been posted to a station where horse-sickness was rife. Sheba was supposed to be Arab, and certainly she was a lady of parts, but her stature was such that she must have had blood in her other then Arab. I did not ride that fine horse for long, as I was soon posted to Kakamega, one of the hottest forest areas in Kenya, and I could not take her with me, and so once again she changed hands, passing to another Forester. I did, however, during that short time obtain a horse allowance from the Government. It was a great triumph, for even then horses were being replaced by Land-rovers, and officialdom often frowned upon those who were of the opinion that they could get around better by riding upon a horse.

I did not own another horse until 1963, the year of Kenya's Independence, when, as a Forester at Nandi, I was given a horse by a Forester leaving the country. She was Thella, undoubtedly the fastest pony I ever owned, but no jumper, a fault in forest areas. Thella was a polo pony, with a mouth as hard as iron and the ability to turn on a sixpence. She could, and often did, stop so suddenly that unless you were ready, and prepared to fling arms around her neck, you were deposited in the bushes. She made me a much more accomplished rider, able to ride standing in the stirrups for long hours, just like those legendary cowboys.

There is a lovely story of a new District Officer at Nandi, who pestered me for a long time to let him go for a ride on Thella, and eventually I relented. Half an hour later the pony came galloping back riderless and I went in search of the rider. He was rather a bumptious type who thought he knew everything in life, including how to ride horses. It was most amusing watching him limping along, both hands clutching his back. Later that day I overheard Gertrude Annie describing the downfall of the great one to one of the servants. Gertrude Annie never did trouble to learn much Kiswahili, but her mixture of Swahili and English always saw her through. The end of her narrative proclaimed: . . . 'and he *rudi* [returned] on his feeties'. When I was finally posted from Nandi, I could not take Thella with me and I gave her to the Stocktheft Unit; I do not doubt she did sterling work galloping down cattle rustlers.

Treetops was burned down by the Mau Mau in 1954, and soon afterwards the same gang attacked the Polo Club. They succeeded in destroying the stables, but fortunately no ponies were inside. The clubhouse, being of more substantial material, survived. I am indebted to Eddie Fernandes of Timau for information regarding the old Nyeri Polo Club. When he invited Gertrude Annie and me to a polo tournament near his home he brought along with him the Club's dog-eared minute-book, and I studied it in the car by the touchline as the ponies thundered past. It was a lovely day in a setting of vast, rolling ranchland with the snow-covered Mount Kenya as a close backdrop. May it always stay like that and remain beautiful, not developed by 'settlement' like so many other places in Kenya. Though most of the players and officials were Europeans a few were African, a happy omen for the future.

Eddie Fernandes has told me the story of his presentation to the Queen during her 1983 return visit. It was at the Intercontinental Hotel. He reminded her that in 1952 he had helped her to mount the horse she had gone riding on before breakfast on the Windleys' farm. Not only did she remember the incident but she also remembered the name of the horse— Canasta.

When the stables of the Nyeri Club were burned down by Mau Mau soon after the Queen left in 1952, the Emergency had not yet been declared. As a state of 'civil disturbance' did not officially obtain, the insurance company paid up in full. Four oxen, which would have been used for carting fodder and for pulling the huge lawn-mower, were destroyed, along with 108 unoccupied stables.

At the Club's 1952 annual general meeting it was revealed that, as a result of the fire, coupled with the cancellation of so many meetings, the revenue-over-expenditure figure came to just 26 shillings. Yet the Club bravely carried on. A few weeks before the next annual general meeting, ie on 28 March 1953, the clubhouse itself was burned down, and the meeting had to be held in the newly built stables. There were no tournaments at all in 1954 because of intense Mau Mau activities, and guards had to be stationed on the site at all times. In 1955 it was proposed that a new clubhouse be built of galvanised iron (to make burning difficult), and that twenty new stables be built, as many horses were having to be picketed. With the financial aid of other clubs this was carried out.

By 1964, membership had dropped to nine, largely because of the exodus of so many European farmers after Independence, and it soon became obvious that the Club would have to be wound up. The land had always been 'Crown' and had been rented from the Government. The building material was sold to local farmers, debts were cleared, and the minutes of a meeting held on 16 November 1964 recorded that the small amount of money left would be spent on a dinner at the Mount Kenya Safari Club, to be followed by a dance at Nanyuki Sports Club. So ended the short but hectic life of the Nyeri Polo Club.

Sylvia Richardson was head of the women's section of the Club, and after the fire she was given a number of enlarged framed pictures of that historic 1952 match, which hang on the wall of her dining-room. Sylvia is no longer young, and she lives alone. Often she finds herself looking wistfully at those scenes of an era in Britain's colonial history that can never return.

The land on which the Nyeri Polo Club stood was eventually sold to Chief Jonathan. All that is left today is the concrete floor of the clubhouse and a small group of eucalyptus and cypress trees that had been planted for shade and to act as a wind-break. African children can often be seen tending goats where once so many Britishers gathered. Sometimes there are cows—hump-backed Boran cattle whose bells around the neck tinkle as they graze. Every afternoon and morning when I am on Treetops duty, I take tourists past the barren site. Usually I explain to those in the vehicle the history of that desolate scene, but many must pass in total ignorance. When Queen Elizabeth came past in 1983 that very efficient African driver who sat alone with her could have told her much. But then, in 1952 he would not even have been born.

In 1977, when I went to India as the guest of the Government of India, I went to Darjeeling, and was taken to the Tea Planters' Club. I looked at the trophy heads of big game on the walls, and at the scene of pig-sticking. I looked at the bar, and in imagination could see the colonels and captains of yesteryear; I could see the mustachios and the monacles, and listen to the voices, voices that spoke with a plum in the mouth. I do not doubt the Queen saw ghosts too, with the winds off Mount Kenya bringing down whispers of those excited voices at a polo match some thirty years before.

The golf course which today belongs to Nyeri Club was laid out in 1910 by a Mr R. McClure, the District Commissioner, and a Mr Sandbach Baker, who was the Forest Officer. They were the only Europeans in the *Boma* who were interested in golf. Even by 1926 there were only nine Europeans at Nyeri although of course others lived on the farms beyond. The site was cleared by 'volunteer' labour sent in by the local chiefs. Greens as such did not exist, and empty jam tins, 4in (100mm) across, did duty inside the holes.

There is a delightful photograph of those early days, unfortunately not suitable for reproduction, showing ladies putting. They are wearing Edwardian dresses touching the ground and with waists well pulled in. In that same year, 1910, a Mr E. B. Horne, the District Commissioner of Meru, also laid out a golf course, and again he and his assistants were the only players in the *Boma*. The two places were both keen to play a challenge match but, as they were 70 miles (115km) apart, and no vehicles were available for a 'road' that was merely a trail, the match never came off.

Not until 1922 was it possible to start a club, build a clubhouse of cedarwood and shingle roof, and create greens and a proper eighteen-hole course. Our next clear picture of the club comes from the pen of a Mrs

Barbara Simpson, now living at Watamu on the Kenya coast. In 1926 and 1927 she was attending school at a place called Moya Drift. (Funds had been raised by a farmer's wife for a school for twelve children as a means of educating her own children. The education of settlers' children was a great problem at that time.) Some were sent to England but not all settlers had the money for this. Once a week the children at Moya Drift were sent to the Nyeri Club where they participated in the rites and activities of the Girl Guides, Brownies or Cubs. Barbara remembers the club as a long wooden building on piles, with a kitchen at one end. All wooden buildings were on raised piles at that time because of the ravages of white-ants (termites). Afternoon tea was made for all present by two children in rotation and Barbara remembers that once, when it was her turn, she and her companion made it so strong that half had to be poured on the ground and the huge kettle filled up again. After tea was over the adults usually gossiped whilst the children played on the grass outside. Often they had competitions rolling down the steep slope. She remembers how the return home by car in the dark was always exciting. In the dry season it was very dusty. In the rains they slid in every direction in the mud, and at all times they saw eyes in the forest, animals crossing the road ahead, or great herds standing on the plains. Once they had just left after games of rolling down the bank when the car lights revealed a huge male leopard standing on the path.

In 1943 the old wooden structure was replaced by a spacious stone building with red tiles. Today Africans, Asians and Europeans play the course in roughly equal numbers.

I mentioned earlier that the nearby Nyeri churchyard has many gravestones bearing inscriptions indicating that the deceased was killed by elephant, rhino or buffalo. (There are also a number of victims of the Mau Mau buried there.) I have no details, and memories now are faint, but I know one farmer was killed by a rhino as he was valiantly trying to distract it from his wife. Where the old police station and the prison once stood, and where there is now an infant's crèche, just across the road from the Club, an old African was killed long ago by an elephant, and the local Wakikuyu made a song about it, but I can elicit no details, for the man who told me is now dead. There is also the story of a man being killed on the golf course itself by buffalo. Stories of big game incidents from the 1960s onwards, however, are much easier to verify. The same week that I took over Kiandongoro Forest Station a dozen miles further up the mountain, in August 1960, an African woman was killed by a rhino when returning to her home bent double beneath a load of firewood. A few days later the

Treetops' first casualty. A young bull elephant, caught up in a poacher's snare and maddened by pain, is shot by the hunter before it can attack any of his seven guests. (*Block Hotel Archives*)

same animal charged through a herd of cows, killing one and wounding another. A few months after that a very old man, who was spending the night in a small hut on the edge of a maize shamba to guard it, speared a leopard by the glow of his tiny fire as it stepped inside.

Conflict between man and wildlife has always been a feature of the lower parts of the Aberdares. I was involved with the inspection by the National Parks authority and the Forest Department of their mutual boundaries.

One day I could not attend because it was the monthly pay-day and so my boss, Colin Holloway, went. In the afternoon the party was scattered by a charging rhino. Colin was a small man, and consequently the slowest. He was overtaken, hooked and within seconds found himself sitting on the rhino's head, holding on by the long front horn. When Bill Woodley, the Park Warden, returned, it was to find the rhino pirouetting in a cloud of dust with Colin still holding on. He dared not fire his rifle for fear of hitting the man, so on the next turn around he smacked it on the rump with the butt of the rifle. Colin was tossed into a thorn-bush and the rhino departed. I saw Colin next day in hospital, his ears covered with bits of plaster where thorns had taken pieces out. Eventually his wife announced an expected happy event, and at once all the Foresters agreed that rhino horn *must* have some virtue.

One evening a local man, coming out of the Park, decided that Nature must have its way and left his vehicle. Without any provocation he was tackled by a buffalo and quite seriously hurt. He got back into his car and drove slowly and carefully all the way down the mountain until he reached the Nyeri Club. There club members took over and got him safely into hospital where he duly recovered.

Even in the 1970s incidents occurred. The manager of a nearby coffee estate was coming into Nyeri for a friend's party when his car started to give trouble. 'Never mind,' said his host when he finally arrived, 'go home in mine and we will get yours repaired for you and you can return my car later.' Going home in the friend's car, in the small hours, he hit a rhino with a big calf in the Nyeri Forest. As the car shuddered to a halt the youngster smashed in the side. The man escaped, considerably more sober, and succeeded in getting home on foot. Next day he reported the incident to the Game Department, who searched the area. Though the car was a virtual write-off the rhino and its calf were never seen again.

The Clerk at the Abderdare Country Club, whose home is not far from the Nyeri Club, was mauled by a leopard which suddenly jumped out of a bush. He was returning home on leave, and unknown to him this leopard had been chased from one bit of cover to another for hours. Arrows had been fired at it and spears had been flung at it; dogs had chased and barked at it; and it was in just the mood to attack the first passer-by. Fortunately for the Clerk, leopards when harassed rarely push through their attack. It is nice to know that the leopard finally escaped from its persecutors.

The Golf Club at Entebbe, in Uganda, boasts that it is the only club in the world with a rule that allows players to pick up the ball—without penalty—when it has landed in a hippo footprint, but Nyeri Club can boast of having been built in an area providing a probably unique degree of excitement in terms of wildlife incidents.

Nyeri Club's great day came on 12 November 1983 when it was decided to invite the Queen to a display of tribal dancing and school singing. I don't know who actually made the great decision but the Vice-president of Kenya is one of the Club's keenest patrons and a great golfer, and he escorted Her Majesty whenever the President was unable to be present. He comes from the Nyeri area and can often be seen in the Outspan Hotel.

Her Majesty was due to arrive at the club at 5pm. During the day she had been busy inspecting a factory 80 miles (130km) away at Thika, and the road, though tarmac, was good only in parts. And there had been that long climb up *Pole pole* hill, which, in Kiswahili, means 'slowly slowly'. It is so steep that there is no other speed one can go. It was no wonder that, when she did arrive, the Queen looked pale and tired. The Duke was not with her, having left to open a new road around Mount Kenya, a British Government project. As a result the press had gone haring around the mountain, thinking there would be more to see there than in a little country club. They never knew just what they were missing.

Nyeri town turned out in such vast numbers to see the Queen that I had to take Gertrude Annie down early in the car, leave her in a good viewing position, then return the car and proceed back on foot the full length of the golf course to rejoin her. I do not know where the town obtained the long red carpet linking the road to the club steps but I do know what happened when a dust-devil suddenly struck. Spiralling dust storms are a feature of hot weather in the tropics, and can rise without warning. Two police officers in their immaculate uniforms knelt down and blew away the dust for a considerable distance, then patted the fabric smooth before standing up again and desperately trying to pat the dust and crinkles from their trousers.

When the excitement was at its height, and all the children appeared to have arrived, the District Commissioner commenced handing out flags, Kenyan and British alternately, so that each child could hold one. After Her Majesty had signed the visitors' book she emerged from the clubhouse and sat in the centre of a long line of chairs on the club verandah. Before her were the colourful Wakikuyu dancers in their traditional dress, followed by the girls of Tumu Tumu School. The scene was, perhaps, the most beautiful in Kenya, for the last rays of the setting sun were lighting up the snows on Mount Kenya, not so far away. It was a poignant scene too, for she must have thought how vastly different the people before her were from the Kikuyu she had last seen almost thirty-two years before. There are

Tea is served for the few people present by Eric Sherbrooke Walker himself. Note the walls are made of papyrus matting to economise on space. *(Keystone Press Agency Ltd)*

few earlobes hanging almost to the shoulders today, filled with coils of gaudy beads, as there had been then. They were no longer a primitive people. Though the tribal costumes were genuine enough the wearers were educated, speaking very good English, and many would have been working in offices. Though the drums they were beating, the songs they sang and the dances they danced were of the old Kenya, they themselves were of the new, and most would not even have been born in 1952. But it is good to keep alive the old cultures. What has Britain to show today other than a little morris-dancing?

There were no speeches, for speeches would have been a banality. It was the only time I have been present in a mighty gathering of this type in which speeches have not been made. The welcome was in the smiling faces, and in the wonderful words of the songs—words which were so moving that they made the tears glisten on many a hardened cheek. After the tribal dancing came the schoolgirls from Tumu Tumu. Dressed in yellow blouses, brown skirts and white socks they danced and fluttered around on the grass like daffodils in a breeze, like rays of sunshine in a day far spent. They were followed by younger children from other schools, singing in a higher pitch to the tune of that old English favourite, 'In an English country garden'. The words of the songs were wonderfully fitting for a country that has retained all that is best from the influence of another country so very far away. The poignant words and the gestures went unheard and unseen by the world's press, still in the wake of the Duke opening the new road. For the sake of posterity, and so that they will never be forgotten, they are reproduced as follows:

> *A jubilant salute*
> Welcome! Karibu!
> Oh Daughter of our land!
> For you have come back!
> Like a beacon our beautiful land
>   has lured you back.
> Welcome back! That mountain booms!
> Your Royal Majesty, the Queen,
> A gracious and charming sovereign,
> A noble and loving mother,
> With a smile worth a million,
> A mind at peace with everyone,
> A heart overflowing with kindness
>   and tenderness. With open arms
> We welcome you back home.
> Three decades ago a princess you ascended
>   Treetops.
> A queen you descended to your preordained position,
> And a great honour to our land.
> Welcome back! The wind echoes in jubilation.
> We were yet to be born.
> May your stay here be pleasant.
> And may we cherish the memory
> Of this great honour to our Motherland.
>
> Your Royal Majesty,
> Britain and Kenya are not new friends.

It was here in Kenya that you visited
Just before Your Majesty became
The head of the British people.
May this bond of friendship between us
Never wither, fade or die.

Your Royal Majesty,
We wish to send you to Britain,
To the children of that great nation.
Take our message of love and friendship.
For far apart as we may seem to be,
We are but the youth of tomorrow.
Today and the world tomorrow
Will be ours to lead.

And now Your Royal Majesty,
Accept our thanks and humbleness,
As we bid you here farewell.
When back at home, do please remember
Our land—where *jambo* means hello.
Kwaheri is our word for 'bye.
Karibu means please come again.
Thank you and goodbye Your Majesty.

Kenya our country
How many types of game will you find
In a Kenya country forest?
We know a few and we'd like you to see them
Before you leave our country.
Yet we read and hear
Of the thriving ties between ours
    and yours.
Thank you, for the aid you grant us.
Thank you, for the heritage of
Legal and government systems,
Farming, and even religion.
Welcome! Your Royal Majesty.
Welcome to our game parks.
We offer you the best.
As a token of gratitude
You offered a home

To the late Father of our Nation,
    and many other leaders.
Welcome back! Let this be one of
    many more visits.
We proudly proclaim our association
With Britain, our greatest trade partner,
Our friend in need.
Now we pray for continued peace.
Welcome! Karibu! Oh sovereign Queen!
Welcome! Karibu! Oh Daughter of our land!
For you have come back! Like a beacon our bountiful land
Has lured you back! That mountain booms!
Long live Great Britain.
Long live the Republic of Kenya.
Long live the Commonwealth.
Long live the Queen!
God save the Queen!

Welcome to Nyeri Your Majesty
Your Royal Majesty,
Welcome to this our Motherland,
We feel most grateful to you
For agreeing to come to our land, Kenya.
Zebras and buffaloes, lions and elephants,
Cheetahs and bongos, leopards and birds,
Many more you'll see and you'll find out—
Your visit will be wonderful.

How many mountains, rivers and lakes
In this beautiful country Kenya?
We'll tell you of some that we all know that do
    exist in Kenya.
Mount Kenya, Elgon, Aberdares, Longonot,
Tana, Chania, Tsavo, Nzoia, Athi
Lakes Nakuru, Naivasha, Baringo
And the biggest Lake Victoria.

How many races that do
Exist in our beautiful country Kenya;
We'll tell you of some that we all know.

In our motherland of Kenya
Africans and Europeans, Japanese, Americans,
Indians, Arabs, Chinese and Greeks.
We are all guided by one motto,
Peace, Love and Unity.

Perhaps we will never know who thought of those beautiful words, both in English and Kikuyu. Perhaps they were the joint effort of many people. Whoever wrote them, they were inspired—fit for a royal occasion.

When the Provincial Commissioner told me that the Queen had commanded her personal secretary to obtain for her a copy of those words I felt proud and deeply moved; proud to think that our two countries of Britain and Kenya could be so close when both had suffered so much thirty years ago, and deeply moved to think that Kenya had had the wisdom to reject the worst and retain the best of all that she had inherited from the British.

5
A PRINCESS BECOMES A QUEEN

Although this chapter is the most important in the saga of the Queen and Treetops it has proved to be the most difficult to write. Many people have helped me, it is true, but most of those involved are now dead, and records in the press and other media are often at variance. It is based largely on Jim Corbett's little book *Treetops*, Eric Sherbrooke Walker's *Treetops Hotel* and Mervyn Cowie's *Fly Vulture*. In reading them one is struck by the clash of personalities at the time of the Queen's first visit. It was also much in evidence when Her Majesty returned thirty-one years later, when it was, of course, impossible to present all who felt they should be presented, or even to invite them all to the parties, resulting in some bitterness.

There was a lot of bitterness about and opposition to the creation of the National Parks—Royal National Parks as they were called then—and there was also opposition to the reduction of the Forest Reserves to make way for those parks. Mervyn Cowie unquestionably had to bear the brunt of this. His Parks, now such an important national resource, were indeed a Cinderella organisation.

Three people played key roles during the twenty-four hours prior to the Princess' climb up into a tree—the authors of the above three books. It all started when Walker and his wife Lady Bettie decided to invite the royal couple to their little house in a tree during the five-day stop-over made by the Princess and the Duke on their way to Australia. There must have been tremendous excitement and subsequent planning from the moment the message came through that the Princess had graciously accepted. This chapter is centred around the activities of those three people.

It was early January when Walker heard that the Princess was coming to Treetops, and from that moment his anxieties mounted. Not only was he worried about whether animals would appear—all wild animals have a tendency to disappear when they are most wanted—but there was also the

Soon after the Outspan Hotel opened a Witchdoctor arrived and tried to sell an enormous leopard skin. (*Block Hotel Archives*)

question of security of the person, both from animals and from the Mau Mau, which was just starting. Though the state of emergency was not to be declared until the August, plenty of violent incidents had occurred, and the country was full of stories of night meetings in the villages of the Wakikuyu. The British Government, so many thousands of miles away, simply would not believe the reports that were coming out of Kenya, taking the view that the unrest was no more than banditry which could be contained by orthodox methods, but almost without exception the settlers knew it was much more serious. Accordingly Walker arranged for patrols of trustworthy Africans, armed with spears, to patrol the boundaries of the forest for miles, with orders to turn away all they saw in the vicinity. There was also the problem of the press. Though they had been told that it was a private visit and that no photographs were to be taken, about a score had booked into the Outspan, determined to obtain the pictures of the year. Walker realised that it might only take one journalist or photographer wandering into the vicinity of Treetops to drive the animals away and so ruin the royal visit. So he had a long talk with them, and finally they agreed to keep away, a promise every one of them kept.

Eight people were scheduled to spend the night in Treetops, excluding the two African staff. Supplying food etc for a party of that size did not, of course, entail any problems. About midday Lady Bettie, her elder daughter Honor and the family friend Jim Corbett went up to the tree by car with provisions and to ensure all was in perfect order. The African cook and waiter were already there. We know the name of the cook, Ladislaus Ng'ang'a, but not that of the waiter, or kitchen *mtoto* as they were often called at that time. Yet it was the waiter who became the hero of that night, putting out the fire caused by an upturned stove with a wet cloth. And it was the same waiter who was guarding Treetops some months later when it was raided by a gang and all the blankets and utensils were stolen. He was never seen again and Jim Corbett speculates as to whether he was murdered and his bones lay bleaching somewhere in the forest or whether he joined the Mau Mau, possibly under threat of death. Those were terrible days.

Before Lady Bettie, Honor and Jim Corbett left the Outspan Walker made an arrangement that, should any dangerous animals be around Treetops when the royal party was due to arrive, a white towel or pillowslip would be hung out of a window. It must be remembered that only after rising the steep hill and turning the last corner of the bushy path could Treetops be seen.

The drama of 5 February 1952 starts with Jim Corbett waiting eagerly on the Treetops verandah for the arrival of the royal party. The fact that the sun is shining in a clear blue sky is not surprising, for in Kenya February is the dry time, and the sun very often shines from dawn until dusk. At an altitude of 6,500ft (2,000m) there is no humidity, so that the air is often wine-like, hot in the sun but cold in the shade. As the time draws near Corbett becomes restless, and moves down to the platform at the top of the 30ft (9m) steep steps. In his book he describes the clearing as 200yd (180m) long by 100yd (90m) wide, oval in shape—certainly not the vast space we see today. The miniature lake is directly in front of him, studded by tufts of grass, occupying two-thirds of the total area. A salt-lick covers the rest. He does not say that it was a man-made saltlick, but that is what it really was, created by twenty years of application. A solitary rhino was on the saltlick, moving restlessly back and forth as rhino so often do.

Across the water was a stretch of grass (the site of the present Treetops), and beyond that was a hillside of forest containing many big Cape chestnut trees. These were in flower, a glorious expanse of pink. Colobus monkeys, probably the most beautiful monkey in the world, were flitting about in these trees. Their long white flowing tails and silky white mantles over black bodies made them look like some kind of giant butterfly as they cavorted from branch to branch. Only a few of those pink-blossoming trees are left today, but the beautiful colobus still come for the tender young leaves which sprout with the blossom. Further back, the forest stretches to the skyline just as it did in Jim Corbett's day.

He describes the scene as beautiful and peaceful, but he knew that all was not well, for he could hear, but not see, approaching elephants, and the discordant trumpeting sounds they made meant that something was wrong in the family. As the sounds drew nearer the monkeys and the rhino left. Only a solitary heron continued to fish at the water's edge, and a mother dabchick, with a fluffy brood looking—from the height of Treetops —like marbles continued to cruise around. Jim Corbett was worried, and no wonder; the royal couple were due to arrive any time, and it was a question of whether the elephants or the royal party would appear out of the forest first. They had been scheduled to leave the Royal Lodge at Sagana at 1pm and arrive at Treetops around 2pm. It was now 1.30 and a white towel had been hung from a window the moment the discordant sounds of the elephants had been heard. Just a few hours before, Jim Corbett had received the breathtaking 'phone message from Sagana that the Princess would be pleased to include him in her party. He must have felt like I did thirty-one years later when I finally realised that I, and I alone, would be escorting the Queen back to the site of the old Treetops, quite a distance from the new one.

Corbett finally sent one of the two African servants down to the carpark to inform the party of the danger. He knew how experienced these two men were at climbing trees if this proved necessary. As the minutes ticked by slowly, as they do in times of stress, Jim Corbett speculated as to whether the royal party could possibly arrive before the elephants emerged from the forest. Royal parties, however, are often a little late, and soon the elephants began to emerge on a broad front, elephants ranging in size from a huge bull to infants only a few weeks old, and this went on until he had counted no fewer than forty-seven of them. Elephant arrivals at Treetops during the dry month of February are rare, for they love the high ground, where it is both cooler and greener. That so many should arrive together was rarer still. That they should emerge from the forest in the heat of the day, and when a princess was due was little short of a miracle. It soon became apparent that in addition to the big bull there were two younger bulls, and it was the presence of these younger bulls that was causing the discord.

Jim Corbett lived in an era before the African elephant had been studied scientifically. He had been born in India, and knew his Asiatic elephants as well as any person living. But the Asiatic and African elephants are very different from each other, having different habits and a different social structure. The African elephant has a matriarchal society, with an old cow leading at all times—giving out messages of intent in the form of, for example, throat rumblings and ear movements—even when a breeding bull has moved into the herd. When control work is being carried out today (once poaching ceases the next problem is too many elephants), the matriarchal cow is always shot first, whereupon the whole herd bunches in confusion. Jim Corbett believed the big bull was in musth (frenzy), in the manner Asiatic elephants go into musth, and was simply there as a breeder. The two smaller bulls may have been competitors for the cow or they may have been of that age when all young bulls are thrown out of the herd. The big bull may have been simply following the matriarchal cow's example in chasing them away. I have watched young bulls being chased out of the herd many times, and it often takes weeks before they finally realise that they are not wanted. Sometimes the old cow will run such an animal along like a wheelbarrow, digging her long thin tusks into each buttock. And sometimes she makes a miscalculation, and there is a big red patch under the tail, where a tusk has missed its mark. Such young bulls will be ostracised by the entire herd until they finally take to hanging around the perimeter, looking utterly miserable, until they leave and join with a few other youngsters in a like predicament.

Whatever the cause, this big bull was unquestionably annoyed with the two young bulls, and he chased them around in a circle, and finally in the direction of the path along which the royal party was due to arrive. Jim Corbett also records that one of the young bulls bore a small wound in the shoulder from the constant jabs. No wonder the man was biting his nails as the minutes dragged slowly by. Then he records catching sight of a man coming around the corner of the forest path carrying a rifle at the ready, followed closely by a small trim figure which he recognised instantly as the Princess, though he had never met her. As they came into full view of Treetops, with its milling herd of elephants around, they came to a halt.

At this stage, apparently, Jim Corbett could contain himself no longer. Seizing his heavy rifle he dashed down the steps. For some minutes a big cow elephant, presumably the matriarch of the herd, had been standing placidly in the shade of the fig-tree, flapping her ears contentedly and showing no signs of wanting to move. Between the cow and the path was a screen of cut bushes intended to help visitors remain hidden when arriving, but this had been trampled upon until it was a screen only in name. Presumably he contained his anxiety sufficiently to tiptoe carefully past this cow without agitating her. Then he reached the Princess, who is recorded as smiling her greeting and passing him her camera and handbag before walking unhurriedly to the steep ladder and climbing to safety. There are times when a formal presentation is neither necessary nor desirable. After ensuring that the Duke safely followed the Princess, Sherbrooke Walker and Windley returned to collect the second half of the royal party—Commander Parker and Lady Pamela Mountbatten—from the place in the forest where they had been left, at the foot of a ladder.

It is recorded that no sooner was the Princess sitting safely on the viewing verandah than she started filming the elephants below—the first she had ever seen in Africa—with hands that remained perfectly steady. Later the position of the footprints of that old cow elephant was measured by various people, and none made it more than ten paces away from the foot of the steps.

We must now leave Jim Corbett, Lady Bettie and her daughter Honor entertaining the royal couple in Treetops, and go back to what happened at the carpark and to those other central figures in the drama, Sherbrooke Walker and Cowie. Walker was the planner; Cowie the unseen, unheard, backstage figure about whose exploits I knew nothing until I read his book *Fly Vulture*.

When reading Sherbrooke Walker's description of the arrival of the royal party at the Treetops carpark one is impressed by the fact that two people were armed with heavy rifles (himself and Windley), and that he immediately handed a 'spare' rifle to the Duke. Presumably they would all be doubles for the double was by far the most popular big-game rifle at that time. That the Duke was a good rifle shot is well known, for he had hunted in India and in Nepal. Such heavy protection was certainly justified on the grounds of the lawlessness prevalent in Kenya at the time, but not on the grounds of protection in dense forest against wild animals. Jim Corbett, who had his own heavy rifle in Treetops, was a lone hunter. In all of his six books there is no mention of a companion hunting with him, and there is no more dangerous animal to hunt than the man-eating tiger. Over and over again he emphasises the problem of protecting other people.

Danger from wild animals in thick cover always comes when least expected. It explodes. In those days rhino were almost as numerous as buffaloes are today. Elephants usually, though not always, tower above the

Many stamps have been issued to commemorate Princess Elizabeth's stay in Treetops. Perhaps the best was that for 50 shillings printed for her Silver Jubilee in 1977 and which quotes the words of Jim Corbett. *(Block Hotels Archives)*

undergrowth, and so give a warning of their presence; also, their stomachs are often noisy. Both rhino and buffalo can come charging out of thick cover with a suddenness that has to be experienced to be appreciated. As an example of what can happen when too many people have rifles, I will cite the shooting of a Forester in 1956, a week or so before I arrived back in the country. Three Forester friends and a tracker set out one morning from Londiani to hunt buffalo. They were charged by a bull from dense cover and one man was shot dead. In spite of intensive enquiries it was never discovered who fired the fatal shot, for the bullet passed through the body and was not recovered. It is doubtful whether either of the two survivors knew himself, for, in those seconds before the buffalo arrived, eyes would have been glued upon the spot where it was expected to appear, to the exclusion of all else. In proof of this I myself shot my favourite dog out of a pack of four without even seeing him. I was carrying out buffalo control for the Government with a trusted companion and a calf was shot. The cow must have been standing just behind cover, for she turned on me suddenly. I shot her in the head as she hooked, but never saw the dog as he jumped out of the grass, and both fell dead at my feet to the same bullet. My best friend of those hunting days shot his companion through the fleshy part of the arm when hunting buffalo. They were charged in thick cover and his companion jumped off the path right into the line of fire. By incredible luck there was no permanent damage.

As the second half of the royal party walked slowly up the steep Treetops hill, led by the escort Edward Windley and guarded on either flank by Walker and the Duke, the discordant trumpeting of the elephant bulls became so loud that Walker decided the danger was too great, and stopped. Lady Pamela Mountbatten and Commander Parker, being unarmed, were left standing at the foot of two trees with ladders, and requested to climb the moment a dangerous animal appeared on the path. The reduced party then proceeded but, as they neared the crest, the noise so intensified that Walker again halted the party and asked the Duke for his opinion as to whether they should proceed, and upon seeing his nod of agreement they carried on to the last bend and the point where Jim Corbett finally saw them.

We now come to the part played by Col Mervyn Cowie, then Chief Executive of the newly formed Royal National Parks authority, and John Hayward, Warden of the Aberdare Royal National Park. John Hayward had spent months fixing the new artificial moon at Treetops, a Heath-Robinson affair connected to an engine hidden deep in the forest and so arranged that the light could be increased or decreased gradually. In those days they were obsessed by the belief that a sudden light would scare away animals due to rampant poaching. Edward Windley was the Provincial Commissioner stationed at Nyeri, and when Cowie had called upon him in his office he had been shattered to be told that neither Cowie nor Hayward would play any part in the royal arrangements, that Windley and Walker would be the joint escorts, and that it was on the direct orders of the Governor, an order that brooked no argument. Cowie had brooded a long time over the injustice of this, and had even asked Jim Corbett for his respected opinion as soon as he had learned that Jim was to be a member of the royal group. He had finally gone back to the Provincial Commissioner and told him that he and Hayward intended to patrol the path in advance as a duty. The answer had been: 'All right, but don't show yourselves!' As Cowie puts it in his book, they would have to act as fugitives in the land which they were in charge of.

In his talk with Jim Corbett in the Outspan Hotel the two had come to an agreement that, once ready to carry out the unseen patrol, Cowie would let Corbett know by approaching Treetops and waving a white handkerchief. Cowie makes the point that, though he respected Windley as an administrator, he had no faith in him as a hunter. I do not doubt he was right, for, years later, I was to come up against the same sort of thing in the Forest Department. Out of the hundred or so Foresters up and down the country not more than half a dozen possessed a diploma as proof of their qualifications. The rest had been given two-year contracts, usually by virtue of being the right people in the right place at the right time. If the budding Forester had been in the Indian Army, had a title, talked with a plum in the mouth and wore a fierce mustachio or a monacle, his chances of acceptance were greatly enhanced.

When the Princess returned as Queen thirty-one years later, some members of the press were to make assertions such as that sharpshooters were positioned behind trees. That was rubbish, of course. Apart from anything else it would have been highly dangerous.

Some hours before the royal party was due Cowie and Hayward entered the forest and joined the Treetops path, presumably at a point about where the crossroads are today. Hayward took the lower half to patrol and Cowie the upper, and when the latter reached Treetops he gave Corbett the handkerchief signal, which was acknowledged. He then returned to the point where he and Hayward had parted and sat down under a bush to await the arrival of the royal group.

It was whilst resting thus that he heard a crackling of twigs and, upon standing up, was amazed to see a bull elephant only a few yards away, perfectly motionless and bleeding slightly from a cut on the left shoulder. This was the elephant that Jim Corbett describes as having been chased by the old bull around Treetops and towards the path along which the royal party was expected within the next half-hour. Elephants are like that, they appear like ghosts when least expected. That he had recently been fighting and was doubtless in a bad temper was clear. That he must be moved before there was trouble was equally obvious. How to do it without using a rifle was not so obvious as animals must only be killed in a National Park as a final solution, and the elephant gun was so loud it would ruin viewing for many hours.

Mervyn Cowie finally solved the problem by using a hunter's trick that is easier to explain than to carry out. He rubbed a small pebble (stones are very difficult to find on the Aberdares) under an armpit and then flung it beyond the elephant. No sooner did the elephant get the human scent from that pebble than it charged towards it and carried straight on, crashing through the undergrowth and trumpeting its wrath loudly. There was no doubt whatever about its feelings towards man, and that it had indeed

Elephant herds of over a hundred were often seen at the old Treetops just as they are today. Buffalo, however, were much more rare. *(Mrs Audrey Highwood)*

posed a very real danger. Once again Cowie hid in the bushes and waited, and eventually the royal party arrived, and from only a few feet away he watched them. Then he arose for the second time that afternoon and continued back down the path until he joined up with Hayward, whom he told about the elephant episode. They both followed behind the royal party, making sure they were not seen.

On the flat ground near Treetops, they were horrified to see the huge cow elephant standing beneath the fig-tree, and they lay down together, the sights of their rifles lined up on its brain. Cowie whispered to Hayward that they would fire only if she stepped over that trodden-down wall of brushwood. Fortunately that moment never came, and so nobody ever knew that those two most dedicated men had ever been there—probably the two best rifle shots present that day, men whom officialdom had told to keep out of their own forest. It is good to know that both Cowie and Hayward were presented next day.

Now we move back to Treetops to learn of all the wonderful things that happened that day. That forty-seven elephants visited Treetops is a wonderful thing in itself, for—as observed already—February is the traditional dry time when all elephants on the mountain go up high, where it is both greener and cooler. That they stayed so long and put up such a wonderful show of elephantine behaviour is remarkable. Jim Corbett

90

describes their performance in his fascinating small book. I suppose to a man who has watched it night after night most of his life on two continents it is what the vulgar call 'old hat', but to a young girl fresh from England seeing elephants for the first time in her life it must have appeared as some wonderful dream.

The feeding of baboons with sweet potatoes is innocently described, but there is no innocence in baboon behaviour today, for they steal anything they can lay their hands upon, and can open doors and windows without any trouble.

When it was announced that tea was ready, the Princess is recorded as having said: 'Oh, please may I have it here. I don't want to miss one moment of this.' Fantastic nights like that still do occur at Treetops, as I, who have worked there so long, should know; but for every such night there are a dozen that are not quite so exciting.

Jim Corbett then goes on to describe the killing of a water-buck bull—by another in a fight—the mounted head of which hangs in perfect condition in the Outspan to this day. In all my years at Treetops or at the Ark I have never witnessed such a thing, though I have watched a number of fights to the death between animals of the same species, including one between two water-buck bulls that would most certainly have ended in death had not a tourist decided she could stand no more and screamed. I was bringing down a party of ten in a minibus that morning, when the fight started at the top of the valley. Both were fine bulls, with a big spread of horns, but one was slightly larger than the other; the larger one had the advantage of the higher ground, and drove his smaller antagonist remorselessly downhill. There is a crossroads here, and where a culvert fails to cope with flood water a small lake forms during the rainy season. The smaller beast was valiantly contesting every inch of the ground, and the clashing of horns proved it, but eventually he was driven into the water with a great splash.

There the battle continued for a while as fiercely as ever, but now the smaller animal was weakening, and soon he was knocked down so that his head was underwater. Every time he lifted it he was knocked down again, and eventually bubbles showed that he was in trouble. At that stage the lady tourist leaned far out of the window and started to scream, and the startled victor dashed madly away. Slowly the loser recovered, staggered to his feet, and splashed out.

It was understandable, that scream to save a water-buck from drowning, but it was wrong. Maybe today there are water-buck calves sired by a bull of lesser stature that would not be there had a lady controlled her emotions.

In describing the scenery at Treetops Jim Corbett makes no mention of Mount Kenya, the glorious mountain which dominates the land today. One can only assume that there were taller trees growing behind, or branches of the fig-tree itself, which obscured the view. All his enthusiastic descriptions of scenery are based on the Aberdares which faced Treetops, and the 13,000ft (4,000m) heights of Sattima and Kinangop.

Jim Corbett then tells of his conversation with the Princess, how he told her how distressed he had been to hear of her father's illness, and how pleased he had been to learn of his recovery to the point where he could again go grouse shooting in Scotland. King George VI had suffered a long illness, and had only just recovered from an operation. There have been stories to the effect that he was dying, that he and his daughter both knew it, and that she therefore should not have gone on her holiday. Such stories Jim Corbett had also heard and did not believe. There are always some people who are prepared to believe the worst, and it is on the gullible that the press thrive. It is interesting therefore to read what Sherbrooke Walker himself had to say about it. Apparently his brother-in-law was in Buckingham Palace on the same night that Princess Elizabeth was watching the elephants at Treetops and he listened to His Majesty planning a shoot for the morrow, a morning that he never saw, for he died quietly in his sleep a few hours later. Under such circumstances it is inconceivable that either could have had the slightest suspicion that they would not meet again.

It was a moonlit night, though not a full moon, and it is noticeable that Jim Corbett makes no mention of the 'artificial moon' that Hayward had been at such pains to install. Certainly he makes a point of mentioning how dark it was after the moon set, and one is compelled to the view that, in the absence of Hayward, nobody could operate it efficiently. After the moon had set, which was long after normal bedtime, Jim Corbett sat on, guarding the steps, at the top of the first flight, where a small landing allowed a pause before the final climb into the building. On his knees he cradled his heavy rifle. He had sat in trees in India all night countless times, but now he felt it was both a pleasure and an honour. There was the possibility of a leopard climbing those steps. There was even the possibility of a Mau Mau gang, but over and above this was the fact that it is extremely difficult to fit eight people into three double rooms plus a slip of a room made for the hunter. Sherbrooke Walker says in his book that he wandered through the building during the night. I should imagine he was short of a bed too.

That leopards will climb man-made structures and take advantage of a

Busy scene beneath Treetops as the seven guests descend in the morning. Note the winch for lifting up the steps at night and for handling baggage. By 1952 the steps were no longer raised on the grounds of fire hazard but these are the same steps Princess Elizabeth was to climb. *(Block Hotels Archives)*

convenient platform is a well-known fact. When I was the Forester at Meru by predecessor had made for himself a platform in a tree, and had shot a few animals from it. I spent a number of evenings there myself, and once, when I climbed up, found a leopard had ruined it by leaving there a bush-pig. Leopards leave their kills until they are fairly high before returning, and that pig showed every sign of being just ready for him to enjoy.

Delightful anecdotes concerning the Royal Family are as common as they are charming. Jim Corbett describes how when dinner was announced at 8pm they all trooped into the dining-room which had been laid for seven people (Lady Bettie would be serving). Cushions had been placed on the hard benches for the royal couple, but the Princess asked Corbett to sit between them and that had meant the Duke sitting on the hard wood. This he had done.

An incident occurred after dinner, when coffee was being made. A spirit lamp on the table caught fire and was swept onto the floor. The waiter mentioned earlier put it out. Over-pumping usually causes spirit-lamps to catch fire and makes them very dangerous. Corbett says it was a 'grass-matted floor'. That would be sisal, a Kenya-grown product used extensively in making mats. After dinner they sat out in the fading moonlight and saw no fewer than nine rhinos on the salt-lick, lurching and grunting and making those extraordinary mouse-like squeaks that only rhino make. Since then of course the poaching of rhino has reached such a level that few now remain on the mountain, in spite of the fact that many have been tranquillised outside the Park and translocated into it.

Jim Corbett comments that throughout his night-long vigil no more animals arrived, and that all he heard was the call of hyena, the bark of a baboon and the cry of a tree hyrax. The pattern of early activity followed by silent nights is still with us today. He shaved as soon as it was light and then entered the main building, where he found the Princess sitting in the viewing verandah holding a light meter to ascertain whether she could start filming. The fight which followed between two rhino was the sort of thing that occurs whenever two rhinos meet; its purpose is to create and maintain hierarchy and it is seldom serious. The horn of the rhino, however, is a deadly weapon, and it only requires one thrust in the right place to kill and deaths do sometimes occur.

The royal party left, after a traditional English breakfast, when Windley and his escort appeared. The walk down to the carpark was uneventful, as it usually is at that time of day, and as Sherbrooke Walker shook hands with the excited young Princess, now Queen though unaware of the fact, he uttered a short farewell speech which should go down in history: 'If you have the same courage, Ma'am, in facing whatever the future sends you, as you have in facing an elephant at ten yards, we are going to be very fortunate.' The Princess is recorded as having smiled, and the Duke laughed, but within hours the royal couple were back at Sagana Royal Lodge where the Princess was informed by the Duke that she was no longer a princess but a queen, and indeed the British were very fortunate that their Queen *had* the same courage.

When it was all over, and the royal car glided away, the new Queen of England leaned out of the window, waved vigorously, and called 'I will come again', little knowing how long it would be before she would be able to keep that promise.

In the chapter 'A Queen Returns', the reader will be told how, when she returned, it was not elephants but buffaloes, the most dangerous animals in Africa when fully aroused, that blocked the royal path, and that the Queen showed the same courage.

Next day the Treetops log-book was taken to Jim Corbett at the Outspan for him to fill up and sign and, after entering the names of the party and the details of what had been seen the previous night, he added the following: 'For the first time in the history of the world a young girl climbed into a tree one day a Princess, and after having what she described as her most thrilling experience she climbed down from the tree the next day a Queen—God bless her.' That message, in ink and in a firm hand, can be read to this day.

It is now part of history that the young Princess was told of her father's death soon after the royal party arrived back at the Sagana Royal Lodge by the Duke, that she cried a little, but that she soon put on a brave face for the public. What is not so well known is the remarkable sequence of events leading up to that poignant moment. His Majesty King George VI had died during the night, and a coded message had been sent to Government House, Nairobi, soon after. That message, however, could not be decoded for some time, as the Governor of Kenya, Sir Philip Mitchell, was on a train bound for Mombasa, and he carried with him the code book required to decode all official telegrams. It was some time before Mombasa and the Governor could be contacted, and the contents of the telegram sent back to a stunned Nairobi.

When the news was flashed to the Outspan at Nyeri the only person there who could handle it was Granville Roberts, a reporter with the *East African Standard*, Kenya's only newspaper at that time. Granville Roberts was told he must ensure the news reached the royal party. He intercepted

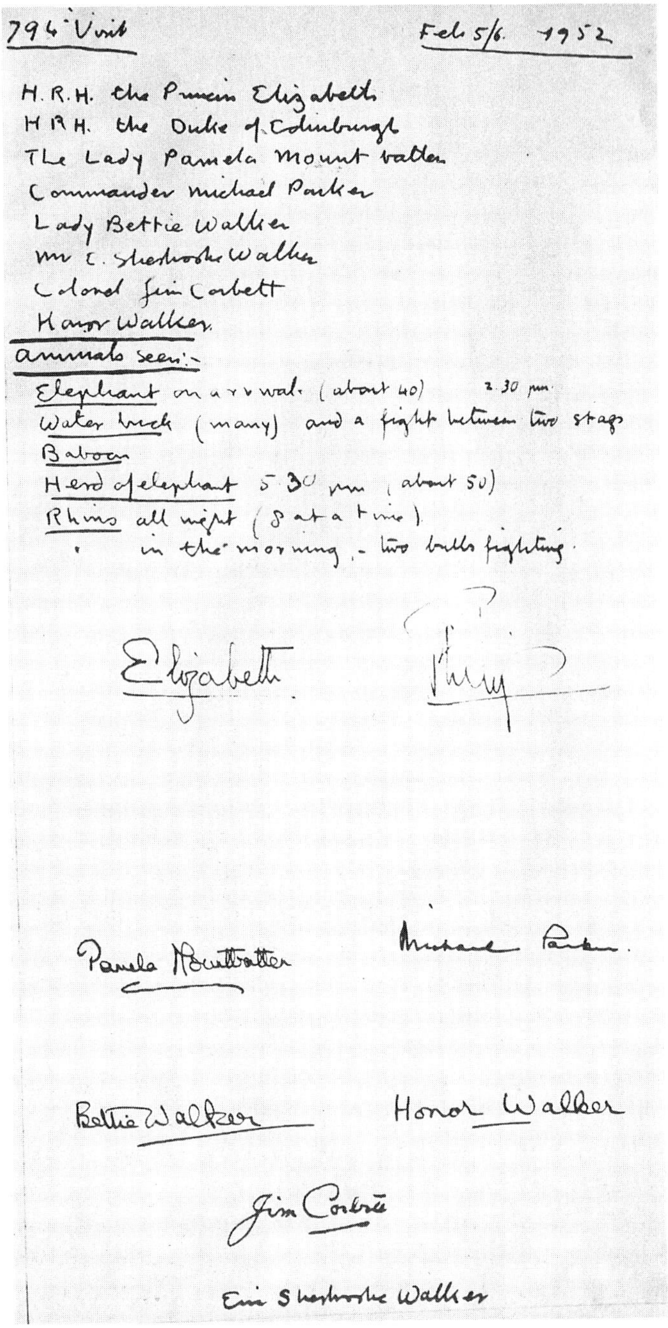

794 Visit   Feb. 5/6. 1952

H.R.H. the Princess Elizabeth
H.R.H. the Duke of Edinburgh
The Lady Pamela Mount batten
Commander Michael Parker
Lady Bettie Walker
Mr E. Sherbrooke Walker
Colonel Jim Corbett
Honor Walker.

<u>animals seen:-</u>
<u>Elephant</u> on arrival. (about 40)   2.30 pm
<u>Water buck</u> (many) and a fight between two stags
<u>Baboon</u>
<u>Herd of elephant</u> 5.30 pm. (about 50)
<u>Rhino</u> all night (8 at a time)
        ,,   in the morning. - two bulls fighting.

Elizabeth   *Philip*

Pamela Mountbatten   *Michael Parker.*

Bettie Walker   *Honor Walker*

Jim Corbett

Eric Sherbrooke Walker

A princess becomes a queen. A record of the night of 5 February 1952 when Treetops was to be honoured by the presence of Princess Elizabeth. *(Block Hotel Archives)* the Private Secretary to the Princess, Lt Col Martin Charteris, just as he was about to leave the Outspan to go with the escort to Treetops and finally on to Sagana Lodge. All Charteris could say upon reading the curt message from Nairobi was: 'This is too awful for words.' Charteris then contacted Prince Philip's equerry Lt-Col Michael Parker at Sagana Lodge, but Charteris insisted there must be confirmation from Buckingham Palace before the Duke could be told. Perhaps he was haunted by the possibility of a mistake and its dire consequences. Accordingly all lines between London and Nairobi were cleared and eventually the confirmation came through.

It is strange how people rise to the heights of diplomatic speech when they have to. We have that short speech by Sherbrooke Walker to Her Majesty, the words written in the Treetops log-book by Jim Corbett, the flash of intuition by the author when he felt he had to reassure Her Majesty about the buffalo bulls and called them just 'retired old gentlemen'. Now we have the words of Martin Charteris, the Princess' private secretary, over the telephone from the Outspan to the Royal Lodge at Sagana. He had to inform Lt-Col Michael Parker that His Majesty King George VI was dead yet he was terrified that listening ears might intercept and let the country know too soon, or even that the whole thing might be some monstrous mistake. 'Mike,' he said, 'our employer's father is dead. I suggest you do not tell the lady until the news is confirmed.' That was diplomacy at its very best.

After the news had been confirmed by Buckingham Palace, Parker tapped on the door of the room where the royal couple were resting after their wonderful but not very restful night at Treetops, and called the Duke outside. The two had been friends for many years, and quickly Parker told him the news. The Duke is reported to have stood silent a few moments; then he turned abruptly, closed the door gently, and told his wife that her father had died peacefully in his sleep during the night.

Although the new Queen had slept so little, and the news caused her to weep, she at once made plans to return to London, and it was most fortunate that a plane could be sent to the small airfield at Nanyuki. By the time she reached Nanyuki by car she had regained her composure, and, dressed in black, insisted on shaking hands with the captain and crew before leaving. Charteris had called an urgent press conference at the Outspan in which he had said: 'I needn't ask you to be kind to them in this terrible hour.' It is to the credit of the press that every camera was pointed downwards as they waved their sad farewells to their new Queen. A raging tropical thunderstorm began to batter Entebbe as the BOAC Argonaut 'Atlanta' touched down, and the flight on to London was delayed slightly.

6
TREETOPS 1952–1985

In the months following Her Majesty Queen Elizabeth's departure from Kenya, until the burning down of Treetops in 1954, so much attention from all round the world focused on the 'little Wendy house in a tree' that constant extensions were necessitated. Not only was another floor added but blankets were used as screens to make more bedrooms, so that on the night of 31 January 1953 a record twenty people spent the night there, as against the eight in the royal party on the previous year. The last group before the authorities banned all further visits on the grounds of security consisted of ten people. It was the night of 4–5 July 1954, and the 1,225th recorded night at Treetops. Not for three years and one day, on 5–6 July 1957, was Treetops to be occupied again. That again was a group of ten— in a new building on a new site.

In the new building piped water and sanitation had, of course, been installed, and the concrete slab covering the septic tank can be seen to this day. Never again was it necessary for water for all purposes to be carried in 4gal *debes* on the heads of porters up that extremely steep hill.

In November 1984 a couple came to Treetops after an absence of more than thirty-two years. They were Jack and Nan Wood, from Yorkshire, and they had visited last on 16 August 1952, only a few months after the royal visit. Jack had been an auditor in the Colonial Government (in which I had served), and so we had much to talk about. When I was a Kenya Forester my office was visited many times by an 'Internal Auditor', or 'Infernal Auditor' as we Foresters liked to call them, but never by a full-blown Colonial. These gentlemen came out from the UK and had the habit of walking unexpectedly into offices and demanding that the safe be opened for inspection. It would be bad enough if the books did not balance, but woe betide any officer whose safe contained a 'Goat Bag'— that little bag of goatskin into which all surpluses went in readiness for the

Treetops in 1952 at the time of the royal visit. *(Block Hotel Archives)*

rainy day when cash was short. One was expected to take all such on charge but refund the latter out of one's own pocket.

Jack remembered arriving in an old safari car escorted by Jim Corbett, who carried a double rifle. Jim Corbett explained that he only went to Treetops when other hunters were not available. It was exceedingly cold and cloudy, as August in the Kenya mountains so often is, and they saw only a couple of wart-hogs before dark. Indeed, they were beginning to wonder whether they would be able to demand their money back when a small herd of elephants suddenly put in an appearance. About a dozen guests were present, amongst them a vociferous old lady who demanded to know in which bed the Queen had slept, but on that subject Jim Corbett refused to talk. The bed Nan was allocated had a huge limb of a tree growing near, over which wads of felt had been glued. In spite of the felt she bumped her head on it, and told Jack he could have that camp bed. She recalled seeing later a glossy magazine showing the same bed and captioned as the one the Queen had slept in. Actually, other records state that Her Majesty was so excited that night that she did not undress but spent most of the night lying on a couch in the viewing lounge.

Nan was intrigued by the rusty old cast-iron stove used not only for making tea but for cooking. When she described it to me I recognised it at once as the Dover stove, a monstrous wood-burning contraption used at every Forest Station where I had been in charge, and also in the army camps of World War II. These stoves had a flat top with a number of circular holes lidded by ½in (13mm) plates which had to be lifted off with a special piece of iron whose end fitted into a slot. The kettle and various pans would sit over these fiery holes. The end section was the fire box, needing constant stoking from a pile of short pieces of wood. The flue was a simple bit of iron piping, and safety measures consisted of the covering of the wall with those ubiquitous flattened *debe* tins. It all sounds impossible I know but very good meals have been made in and on those Dover stoves. To me the thought of them will always bring back memories of toast after a couple of months without seeing bread, toast spread with jams such as guava, pineapple, fig and Cape gooseberry, fruits all grown in Kenya.

As mentioned earlier, the 'plane carrying the royal couple back to London ran into heavy storms. They were widespread, even though it was February. When Nan mentioned the rain to her servant next day he merely shook his head and said it was quite understandable—the Heavens were weeping because a great man had just died.

In January 1953 a Mr and Mrs Highwood and their friends of Limuru, Kenya, went to Treetops for a night, and the photographs they sent me show more than 100 elephants visiting the salt-lick during daylight and make it clear that the trees are suffering and that the glade is expanding. One must remember, however, that at that time the restrictive moat, dug to protect the crops of an ever-expanding population, had not even been started. The herd of elephants would have been migrating, and probably reached the foothills of Mount Kenya the following day. Now such herds are foiled, and are obliged to turn back, but they hang about the area for days, or even weeks, before doing so.

Treetops was now becoming so popular that Sherbrooke Walker was loath to close down, in spite of the ever-increasing danger of Mau Mau attacks, and in the latter days he used two escorts with machine guns in addition to his hunter and heavy rifle. A browse through the log-book reveals officers from various units of the British Army spending a night in Treetops, as well as those from the King's African Rifles. One moonlit night Treetops was the centre of a strange military action, in which bullets whistled through the leaves of Jim Corbett's grand old tree. It was then that, for the one and only time in Treetops' history, the hunter gave the order 'Lie on the floor', instead of the usual 'Up trees'. Security forces were apparently chasing a gang through the forest and, in the bright moonlight, some of the more hotheaded soldiers were firing at anything they thought might be a moving terrorist.

There were American tourists staying at Treetops that night, and Sherbrooke Walker was afraid the incident would reflect badly on his business, but he was delighted to discover that they looked upon the incident as an added bonus to game-viewing. Nevertheless, that was the point when he decided to add machine guns to his other protection. Ever more people wanted to spend a night up the tree, and he hadn't the heart to say no.

Circumstances, however, were moving beyond the control of Sherbrooke Walker, and the situation came to a head when he was informed one day by one of his staff that food destined for Treetops was getting into the hands of the Mau Mau. His informer was extremely frightened, as well he might be, for the penalty for suspected informers was a horrible death. There was no alternative for Walker but to inform the Army and an ambush was laid at the point where the food vehicles entered the forest. The vehicle stopped, two Mau Mau stepped out of the trees, and the food was handed over. At the moment the Army went into action the Mau Mau were somehow warned, and though there was plenty of firing from both sides nobody was hit. Sherbrooke Walker blamed the failure of the ambush on the use of inexperienced soldiers just out from England. Whatever the cause, he did have the satisfaction of learning that his driver was involved, and the man was duly convicted and sent to prison. However, he also had the knowledge that once the two escaped May Mau got back to the main body, retribution was bound to follow. Accordingly all movable items were taken away from Treetops—beds, blankets, crockery, stove, pots and pans. They were not stacked in a vehicle as they would be today, but came

From 1952 until 1954, when Treetops was burned to the ground, security deteriorated. When Treetops was full two 'tree hostesses' were employed, and they were both armed with side-arms and one with rifle. On the right is Honor Walker, and on the left Jane Fermandes. (*Block Hotels Archives*)

down to the trail head just as they had originally gone up—on the heads of porters.

A few days later Mweiga police rang up the Outspan to tell them they could see a column of smoke rising from the forest at the point they assumed Treetops to be. A member of the first army patrol to reach the place has described to me how he found an empty petrol tin amongst the still smoking debris. It has now gone down in history that Sherbrooke

Walker, standing in the ruins of his dream house, with pencil and paper in hand, sketched his plan for a new Treetops. It was not to be, however (at least, not yet), for at that point the Army forbade him to go near the place again.

It was the end of an era. All that was left for Walker to do was to carry back to the Outspan the brass plaque which had to so proudly proclaimed to the world that in the tree a princess had become a queen. Maj Eric Sherbrooke Walker was a man who did not recognise defeat. He knew that plaque would go back and go back it did, though in a different tree. But it was three years and a day before the public could read it again.

There is, incidentally, another plaque commemorating another Princess Elizabeth who became a queen overnight. In 1558 a Princess Elizabeth was sitting beneath an oak-tree in Hatfield Park, Hertfordshire, when one of her courtiers ran up and announced that her cousin Mary ('Bloody Mary'), had died during the night, and that now she was Queen Elizabeth of England.

Only at the very last stages of research were the final pieces of the Treetops jigsaw found.

Honor Sherbrooke Walker, now Mrs Honor Sherbrooke Hurly, elder daughter of Eric and Lady Bettie, now lives in New Zealand. In 1984, during my early research, she was caring for a sick husband. Not until after his death was it possible for her to supply the much needed information.

Not only did Mrs Hurly possess a wonderful memory for detail but she frequently worked as a 'Tree Hostess', in addition to being one of the elect eight who were present that wonderful day in 1952 at Treetops. I am truly grateful for the thirty-six page manuscript she so kindly sent me, and for permitting me to quote from it so freely. Speaking of the indoor lighting she says:

'Light was supplied by two car batteries replaced newly charged each day. For handling these "danger money was paid", because of the risk of an acid leak. Where possible, meals were brought up from the Outspan ready cooked, particularly the evening meal. Hot drinks and breakfast were cooked up there, either on a spirit stove or on the wood stove. Sanitation was of the "thunderbox" type, using the ubiquitous petrol tin. This had a thick layer of sawdust in the bottom, to deaden the sound of liquid on tin . . . an unnatural noise which could frighten off any animals below. The tins were emptied each day well away from Treetops.'

Of the 1952 visit, she records: 'The sanitation arrangements had been improved by replacing the "thunderbox" with chemical, Elsan-type toilets.'

On the arrival of the royal couple that sunny day, 5 February 1952, she has a great deal to say about the dress. It must be remembered February is the hottest time of the year. When they returned in the cooler month of November 1983 both were bare-headed, and *I* of course worried about sunstroke!

'The first glimpse we had of the royal party was of two white hats bobbing along in the bush below. I shall never forget those royal hats; they were not ordinary white hats, they were brilliantly white hats; they were not of ordinary size but great wide-brimmed Stetsons, just the thing to catch the eye of a short-sighted elephant.'

A cow elephant was indeed standing only eighteen paces from Treetops and Sherbrooke Walker, Corbett, and Cowie in their books all emphasise their deep concern about it.

On the mystery of how eight people were fitted into seven beds the mystery is at long last solved, and I quote:

'At 7pm I left Treetops to return to the Outspan hotel for the night, as had been arranged. I noted (in the diary), that Colonel Corbett refused to leave but, as it turned out, he did not occupy a bed. My father and I walked down the path through the gathering gloom, both of us unarmed; it was calm and peaceful, in contrast with all the excitement that had taken place earlier in the afternoon.' In this respect it must be noted that Eric Sherbrooke Walker had been armed with a heavy double to escort the Princess. In Alaska many travellers refuse to carry a rifle in bear country in the belief that it gives undue aggressiveness which the bear can detect and resents. With ladders to hand it could well be that Walker felt something of this.

Finally, Mrs Hurly has a little personal story to tell of her own, and which underscores the intense patriotism felt by every settler who had contact with the Duke and Princess that day:

'In the meantime, I had left the Outspan Hotel at 8am to go back to Treetops. I was stopped at the turn-off from the main road by the police, and was not allowed to go further. A crowd of us waited an hour before the royal car came by. The Duke and the Princess noticed me standing up on the bank by the main road, and turned round to wave to me in recognition. I wish I had been able to take a proper farewell of them.'

It has been said elsewhere the deep concern there had been as to whether animals would appear for the royal visit and that the day before the press had seen virtually nothing. Mrs Hurly muses:

'The only thing to do was to put our extra quantities of salt on the lick, and to pray. My mother had particularly asked the nuns of the Loreto

After two brutal killings close to Treetops, one of a forest guard, who, with a companion was escorting villagers through a dense part of the forest, and the other of two soldiers on patrol, machine guns were added to the normal hunter protection. *(Block Hotels Archives)*

Convent in Nairobi where I had been educated to intercede and pray that the royal visit be a success.'

Our next clear picture of the old Treetops site comes from the pen of Quentin Keynes in his October 1956 article in the *National Geographic Magazine*. The Army had just handed back the area to the police, and with Sherbrooke Walker, Keynes asked the local police chief, John Fletcher, for permission to go back. The answer had been a clear yes—provided they accepted police protection, including that of Fletcher himself. The party which eventually set off consisted of Walker, Keynes, two farm guards, two African police and Col George Jarman, who had been a Treetops hunter-escort for many years. All carried a rifle except Keynes, and they en-countered elephants almost as soon as they entered the forest. It must not be forgotten that the heavy bombardment of Mau Mau hideouts by the RAF during the latter stages of the Emergency had driven many elephants into Forest Department lands. I have personal knowledge of this because they acquired a liking for the bast (underbark) of cypress trees, and I later had the job of cleaning up some of the plantations.

It is interesting to read Quentin Keynes' description of what that burnt fig-tree looked like: a massive 30ft (9m) trunk standing naked, silhouetted against a grey August sky; truncated limbs trailing bits of barbed wire and netting; burned pieces of broken timber. Undoubtedly Sherbrooke Walker thought there was still a possibility that a new Treetops could be built in the remnants of that once proud tree, for when a bull elephant moved up and started to break branches off he grumbled and said he had hoped to utilise the branches again. Then Keynes makes what is to be a very revealing statement. He says the glade appeared to be bigger than when he last saw it, due, he supposed, to the trampling of so many animals. Keynes was not a Forester, but he could see with the keen eyes of the professional writer, and from his pen comes the first indication that the forest was retreating. It was at that stage that rifle shots rang out, and they all really thought that they were going to see some action, but the source of the firing proved to be the two policemen they had left down at the carpark to guard the cars. Apparently elephants had emerged from the forest and the police had lost their heads. Big game on the Aberdares was indeed dangerous at that time and plenty of people had been killed. The animals had been in the centre of the fighting—bombed by the RAF, shelled by the Army, poached by both sides when they needed food. Not for a long time would elephants become the placid creatures of more recent years.

The Kenya Emergency was only declared officially over in 1957, whereupon movement in the forests ceased to be restricted. Sherbrooke Walker was to waste no time in building his new Treetops.

There is only one record available to me dating from the period between the visit to the old Treetops site by Quentin Keynes and the lifting of the Kenya Emergency in 1957, and that comes from the pen of John Cobby, who was one of the District Foresters Officers, and lived in Nyeri. He was my boss in 1960 when I was posted to Kiandongoro. Not many Forest Stations had been closed during the Emergency, though certain areas had been declared closed and were only visited by patrols. A number of Forest Guards had been killed or injured, and even Foresters had been ambushed, but they had always survived. In 1955 John Cobby, together with Bill Woodley, the Warden of the Park, decided to go and see Treetops. In 1955 the area was under the joint administration of the Forest Department and the National Parks authority. Even though it had been gazetted as a Park for some years, because of the Emergency nothing had been done about boundary-marking or buildings, and this was still so even when I took over in 1960. In 1960 I was responsible for fire-fighting and had to provide patrols and their rations. John Cobby's wife went along with them, even though she was pregnant at that time. Life was lonely for a Forest Officer's wife as well as for the officer himself, and the wives often went out in the

Treetops greatly expanded after 1952 to meet popular demand. *(Mr D. Steerman)*

forests as a diversion. On the way to Treetops they were confronted by a rhino and had to run. As a result, John Cobby's wife subsequently lost her baby.

John Cobby, now a senior officer in the South African Government, tells me that the following year Sherbrooke Walker rang him up in his office for suggestions for the building of the new Treetops—Treetops Mk II as it was to be called subsequently. The Forest Department had been experimenting for some years with using cedar bark to cover the outside walls of their Ranger houses. John Cobby was able to tell Walker about this, and the idea was accepted. Mount Kenya was the source of the bark and the huge poles with which Treetops Mk II was finally built, for there is very little cedar growing on the Aberdares.

A lot of other people were to help Sherbrooke Walker build his new Treetops, not least a benevolent bank manager. East African Airways donated seats to furnish the viewing balcony, and the National Parks authority made staff available to camp in the area and maintain security against possible attack by the still angry game animals.

There was now no possibility of building on the old site, for a big bull elephant had pushed over that grand old fig-tree. Surrounding trees affected by the flames had died, and isolated trees tend to tempt elephants to attack. Rocks would have saved the fig-tree no doubt, as elephants do not like rough objects beneath their feet, but during the Emergency no vehicle had been able to get near. So the new Treetops had to be built the other side of the pool, where a group of Cape chestnut and pearwood trees gave distinct possibilities. The other side of the pool also offered a clear view of Mount Kenya, and the sun with which it was favoured in the afternoon was much better for photography.

The same skill was used in constructing the rooms around the trees as had characterised the original Treetops. Tom Arthur was the builder. A pearwood (*Apodytes dimidiata*) grows right through the centre of the building, and today towers more than 20ft (6m) above the roof. This tree very nearly died during the great drought of 1984, and was only saved by constant watering. Other trees through the building subsequently died, but their branches, well padded with sheepskin, are there to this day. The trees growing alongside the dining-room are Cape chestnut (*Calodendrum capense*).

The new Treetops, when completed, had only fourteen beds, but this number was very quickly increased to twenty-two, and since then there have been two major enlargements, which, coupled with the opening up of two stores, have brought the total bed capacity to seventy-three. The alterations, where pieces of wood originally cut out of the huge cedar poles have neatly been returned, can be seen to this day. A different road alignment had to be made, so that vehicles carrying heavy loads had access. New ladders were fixed to trees as a means of escape, and not for some years were they replaced by 'blinds'—shelters of stout circular fencing, with thatched walls and both an entry and an escape opening. I know of no greater thrill than being caught out on a moonlit night when there is a

End of an era. Treetops burned to the ground. The rhino on the left was driven away shortly after this picture was taken by a shot over the head. (*Quentin Keynes, National Geographic Society, Oct 1956*)

power failure and being obliged to take shelter from a big herd of elephants; unless the pachyderms stop to eat the walls away, which can happen when the thatching is new. There is a lovely story from Samburu many years ago in which a guest is supposed to have visited the little thatched-hut long-drop toilet only to see the roof eaten off by an elephant. Unlike the hunter-escorts at Treetops she didn't have a rifle, nor perhaps could she have used it if she had.

Most of the customs which had been such unique features of the old Treetops were maintained in the new, and it is sad that as the years have gone by and new managers have taken over so many of them have been dropped under the pressure of more and more tourists. The new road allowed vehicles to reach Treetops on a much reduced gradient but they only did so when carrying stores that could not be handled by two small hand-carts equipped with rubber tyres. Guests were still expected to walk equipped for the most inclement weather, and the signboard 'No vehicles allowed beyond this point' was respected. Clothing was still expected to be dull and practical, with shoes made for walking. Talking and smoking were forbidden, and baggage had to be small and carried by the staff in the hand-carts. Today there are instances of tourists arriving with trunks as big as themselves and shouting: 'If *that* can't go up to Treetops then *I'm* not going.' We even have cases of people asking: 'Should I take my swimming trunks up to Treetops?'

The new Treetops had gas cooking facilities to replace the Dover stove, and a telephone was installed, together with mains electricity (though a reserve powerhouse was also built). This meant wires going underground. In the enlarged dining-room hurricane lamps had electric bulbs to simulate the real thing. The long tables still had benches on which to sit, but they were padded, not the hard boards the Duke sat on in 1952. A trolley system took the food down the centre of the tables along a trough (I call it an elongated lazy Sue), and the long white table-cloths are whipped off by twisting and pulling one end. I understand that the custom originated in the officer messes of the Indian Army. An air pistol and a catapult were still used to control baboons, and a watchman stood on the highest point of the building to inform the hunter-escort of any dangerous animals near as he escorted in his guests. He had three distinct arm signals—for elephants, rhino and buffalo. A 'hostess' assisted the hunter, and guests still signed a chitty for drinks and then helped themselves! (A lot has changed since 1957. If we carried on like that today the bar accounts would soon be wrong.) A signboard indicated where the path started by which Princess Elizabeth walked to Treetops in 1952. Today a hard gravel road, along which the thirty-six-seater buses travel, obliterates the place. Another feature of the new Treetops was the huge metal spiral fire-escapes that connected the roof to the ground. The roof was flat, a feature ideal for afternoon tea and for wide viewing but difficult to keep watertight, and a firm attitude had to be maintained towards ladies who wore stiletto heels as they would go right through.

The first guest of major importance to stay in the new Treetops was Queen Elizabeth the Queen Mother. (Princess Margaret had been to Kenya during the years when no Treetops existed and the Aberdares were closed.) The Queen Mother came to Kenya in 1959. I did not see Her Majesty at Treetops but I did see her at Kisumu, the port on the shores of Lake Victoria, from where she flew to Entebbe in Uganda, on her way back to London—the same route as her daughter had taken only seven years before.

Thousands of excited Africans lined the main Kisumu road. To the best of my knowledge only one detective walked behind Her Majesty as she strolled along, chatting to those who were fortunate enough to be near and who knew English. (International terrorism had not yet been heard of.) There was one African near who wore little but a leopard-skin cloak which had certainly never been properly cured, for the veins still showed red in the dried yellow skin. He suddenly stepped up behind the Queen Mother and peered down the back of her neck, possibly to see whether she was wearing coloured beads like *his* wife. A look of distaste came over the detective's face as he stepped forward, hooked one finger over the skin, and drew the offender backwards.

Two incidents are recorded concerning the visit of the Queen Mother to Treetops. One reveals the wonderful nature of British royalty, and the other reveals the irresponsible nature of certain sections of the press.

Before the installation of mains electricity, two diesel engines provided power for the artificial moons and room lighting. Both were giving trouble. A message was sent down to the Outspan requesting the services of mechanics, and the best available were sent up—a Sikh and an Italian. By their superhuman efforts power was maintained all through the night, but when the Queen Mother was on the point of leaving both failed and no amount of coaxing would start either of them. So the two mechanics, tired from the nightlong toil, and in their oily overalls, stood on the steps of the powerhouse to watch the Queen Mother walk by, confident that the bushes screened them. But the eyes of royalty miss little, as I was to discover so many years later. The Queen Mother not only saw them but walked over. The Sikh looked down at his feet in embarrassment whilst the Italian shyly stretched forward an oily hand. This the Queen Mother shook, pretending not to notice the greasy overalls, or the stain which would take some time to remove. Royalty at its best.

Next the press at their worst. The Queen Mother displayed a small piece of plaster on an arm, and Walker enquired about it. It was, she said, caused by an insect bite, and she had thought it prudent to cover it against possible infection. Fifteen months later, according to Sherbrooke Walker in his book *Treetops Hotel*, a South African paper brought out a story the author of which said that he had seen a photograph of the Queen Mother at Treetops with a *bandage* on her arm, and that when he had made enquiries he had been told that she had been attacked by a baboon. The Kenya Government, had, he maintained, tried to cover up. No reporters had been allowed to cover the visit and he was only doing his duty in bringing the facts to light.

Close up of the new Treetops. The Apodytes tree growing through the centre is, in 1986, twenty feet higher than this, and protected from big game, is perfectly healthy. *(Geoff Mason Smith)*

Richard Leakey is world-famous as the archaeologist who discovered, in the vicinity of Lake Turkana in Northern Kenya, the oldest fossils of ancient man ever found. What is not so well known is the fact that he once spent a night as a Treetops hunter-escort and was so shattered by the experience that he did not volunteer to stay the following night. He tells the story graphically in his book *One Life.* His Treetops experience took place in 1964 when he was just twenty years old, and had not yet found his destiny as an archaeologist. It would appear that the regular Treetops hunter had fallen sick, and that Leakey was asked to stand in for him. Being short of money, as most twenty-year-olds are, he was attracted by the idea of a night at the posh but pricey lodge, especially as money was to be made at the same time. He was already involved with taking tourists out on photographic safaris and he did not think it necessary to inform his prospective employer that he was in no way a hunter, 'white' or otherwise. After all, he thought, Treetops was just a 'show' place where nothing serious ever happened. He was given instruction as to how to handle the tourists but not a charging elephant.

In 1964 Treetops had a capacity of forty-four beds, and it was a full house that night. The trees were comparatively dense around the building, and the largest of them still had the ladders fixed as escape routes as I had found them in 1960. Leakey says he arrived with the tourists at the carpark and gave them the conventional talk. Putting the heavy rifle across his shoulders, he then told them he was just going to walk around the corner of the path to make quite sure it was clear of dangerous animals. Not for a moment did he anticipate trouble, but soon his ears were assailed by the trumpeting of angry elephants and he saw not only a herd of about fifty around the building but others either side of the path. He returned with much more haste and with the jauntiness knocked out of him, and called his party together. Then he informed them of the problem, though he doubted any of them believed a word he said. He also said he intended to return and, if necessary, would fire a shot into the air to clear the elephants off the path. As a final precaution he then had every small vehicle turned around for a quick getaway if need be.

When he went round that corner a second time, much subdued, it was to find the elephants still there, and showing no sign of intending to leave. So he tiptoed up to a tree which had a good ladder fixed to it, stood at the foot, and fired the heavy rifle into the air. He says the recoil nearly knocked him on his back, and the nearest cow, far from being intimidated, put in a charge. It was, fortunately, a mock charge, and when she had re-turned to the herd, and he had returned to the ground, he went back to his flock of mystified and impatient tourists and explained to them what had happened. He then went up the path for the third time and found that the elephants had taken the hint and departed, and he finally got everybody safely into the tree—meaning Treetops—and eventually all the elephants came back and everyone was happy.

There are normally two hunters employed at Treetops, sharing the duties on a three-days-on, three-off basis, (except for February, which is done two days on, two days off), taking turns to do the odd duty in a thirty-one-day month (and a Leap Year February). That way it is possible to know months ahead whether one will or will not be on duty. During the whole of my eight years at Treetops I have only once had elephants all around the building upon arrival on each day of a three-day duty. I can confirm that it was indeed a nerve-racking experience. Today we have big buses instead of the small vehicles of earlier days to bring up the visitors but all hunters pride themselves on being able to get elephants off the path without either using the biggest bus or firing a shot, but difficult occasions do arise. Just once has a huge bull elephant defied me to stop him feeding on a tree near the Treetops steps and I had to use the big bus. The rifle is reluctantly used—on average about once a year by each hunter. The National Parks authority has to be informed as soon as possible or they might conclude

Eric Sherbrooke Walker and his hunter inspect the old fig-tree after completing the new Treetops. Note the extent of recovery since the burning of 1954 indicating it could have been saved with proper protection. A bull elephant finally pushed it over. *(Block Hotels Archives)*

that poachers were active and send out a patrol.

In May 1968 Treetops Mark II experienced its first really exciting incident when the hunter, Ken Levett, was compelled, at about 3pm, to shoot a cow elephant which charged the last guest he was frantically trying to get into Treetops after an hour of high drama. It was the height of the rainy season and he only had fifteen guests, a not unusually small number for May. A big herd of elephants had been on the salt-lick when they arrived and amongst them was a cow whose small calf had stuck in the mud at the water's edge. The mother charged all who approached, forcing them to retreat. In those days the company used only Land-rovers, so there was no thirty-six-seater bus to drive towards the animal (we have made even the most truculent big bulls give ground with these buses). In the dangerous circumstances Ken decided to wait, and see if the problem solved itself, but after nearly an hour he thought it best to take his guests in two by two, the remainder hiding well back in the 'blinds'.

With the enraged cow only a few yards away he got them all in safely until it came to the last two women. The last blind in those days was under Treetops itself. (Today it is a powerhouse.) One lady stood at the entrance whilst the other was taken the last few paces to the foot of the steps, and at that point the cow decided to charge. That it was the real thing, a different matter altogether from the mock charges she had been making all afternoon, was evident from the ear-splitting trumpet as she gathered speed. There are very few sounds in the African forest more terrifying than the shrill trumpet an elephant makes when it charges. The object of the charge was the small figure standing terror-stricken at the opening of the blind. Ken just had time to race back to her, wheel, and take a brain shot at almost point-blank range. The falling elephant hit the 40ft (12m) upright of the building with such violence that it moved through 20 degrees, and then she became wedged in the blind itself. There is no doubt whatever that she was killed instantly with that brain shot, and that momentum carried her on. Nevertheless Ken Levett put in a security shot, as all good hunters must.

I know of a case where a professional hunter took out a client who shot a buffalo. The client insisted that he must not be backed up, so that he could have the sole credit for the shooting, and he walked over to be photographed, foot on the body in triumph. At that point the buffalo got up and the man is a cripple to this day.

To return to Ken Levett's adventure, at the sound of the two shots the whole herd retreated noisily into the forest but returned half an hour later and did what the poor mother had been unable to do—get the baby out of the mud and onto the bank. As long as a mother in the herd had milk that calf would live. Elephants are like that.

Today a series of huge iron bars sunk into the uprights of the building dramatically reminds tourists that Treetops is not a safari park or a zoo. Unlike some other lodges in the country Treetops has not yet lost a tourist to big game, but only the skill of its hunters will keep it that way. Until the killing of that cow elephant at Treetops there had only been two other incidents concerning dangerous elephants in all of its thirty-six years. Once it was necessary to finish off a young bull which had been badly wounded by poachers and had become a hazard to anybody in the vicinity. The other incident took place when a cow gave birth to a dead calf near the path and the hunter had to fire a number of shots before she would retreat.

It would be about this time that the National Parks authority planted a 3 acre (1.2ha) grove to screen off the lights of Nyeri, now showing through the retreating forest. The idea was sound and, had it been successful, Treetops would have greatly benefitted. The trees chosen were eucalyptus and cypress, both fast-growing exotics but with no other virtues. A ditch was dug, backed up by a split-bamboo fence so that animals would be unable to see the trees, and so would have no incentive to attempt a crossing. Unfortunately one of Kenya's periodic droughts followed; all the trees died and the ditch was eventually filled. Mrs Kay Willson helped with that project, for she was the Outspan florist at that time. I saw the area in January 1969 when I was a Treetops hunter-escort for three months.

It was during my three months as a Treetops hunter in 1969 that Treetops experienced its most dramatic fight to the death since Her Majesty had watched the killing of the water-buck bull in 1952. This time it was between two bongo bulls (the bongo is the most beautiful and rare of all forest antelopes). The two bulls arrived together, as they so often do, at about 11pm and drank at the pool side by side without any indication of animosity. In all situations where two bulls associate, whether it be buffalo, water-buck or bongo, there is no peace until hierarchy has been established, but this is normally done by trials of strength, not vindictive fighting. Once it is known who is the dominant animal and who the subordinate a deep friendship is often established.

As the two bongo stood drinking side by side a buffalo bull came up and jostled them, and in the resulting mix-up one of the bongo jabbed the other, possibly thinking it was the buffalo. From that moment a serious fight was under way, and the buffalo, the cause of the trouble, sneaked off. Animals, like people, have a sense of dignity, and a fight once started does not drop easily. In fact the fight went on until 2am, when the loser died. Bongo have massive horns, and one thrust into an unprotected area like

(*Opposite above*) Twins are extremely rare with elephant and so are malformed tusks of this nature. The matriarchal cow shown here has been a familiar sight in the Treetops area for more than 40 years
(*Opposite below*) The bushpig is seen throughout the Kenyan bush
(*Overleaf*) Thoroughly modernised, the Treetops Hotel is much bigger than the original

(*above*) A bushbuck popular around
Treetops
(*left*) A genet

the stomach can do tremendous damage. Just as the loser collapsed the first hyena came on the scene, brought there no doubt by the sounds of strife—the clashing of horns, grunts, and thudding of the ground. Hyenas had eaten much of the body by morning, but the skull and horns were saved, and hang on the Treetops wall today, together with a series of photographs of the fighting. The trophy head measured 32in (80cm).

About this time the National Parks authority decided to deepen the Treetops pool, using earth-removing equipment. As I have said elsewhere, the pool had been drying up every drought year since Treetops was built. A huge island was created in the centre, but no effort was made to protect it, and eventually elephants pushed it all into the water, resulting in a colossal mud problem and a number of animals getting bogged down when drinking. Sometimes they were pulled out, using boards and ropes; more often they were killed and eaten by hyenas, increasingly the principal predator. The site of the original Treetops suffered greatly during this operation. Not only was there an unawareness of its importance, so that the concrete blocks in which the upright poles had been bedded were pushed around, but many tree roots which would have eventually sprouted were irrevocably damaged.

It was on the island in the pool that I first saw the coypu (or South American beaver), that valuable fur-bearing rodent from South America which was brought into Kenya by a Nanyuki farmer as a means of growing rich, but which escaped and eventually became a nuisance. He had not taken account of the fact that the valuable fur was the result of the ice-cold waters of the Andes; it was hardly an animal suitable for the tropics.

There are many misconceptions amongst tourists about the African elephant and one very dangerous belief concerns its nonchalance. They see a confrontation between an elephant and a cantankerous old buffalo bull in which the elephant spreads its ears, walks backwards a considerable distance, then turns around and walks away. It will do exactly the same with a dove on the ground, and possibly with that legendary mouse. It is all a great bluff (a part of the 'live and let live' mentality of all elephants which Man would do well to emulate), for the elephant can be extremely dangerous once the placid shield it has woven around itself has been shattered, usually by forces beyond its control. A few years ago a rhino was killed by an elephant at another lodge. In that instance the elephant thought that its baby was in danger—a situation no elephant will tolerate.

A friend of mine who worked as a hunter-escort at Treetops in the early 1970s told me an amazing story of a confrontation he witnessed between a cow elephant and a herd of buffaloes. It happened when a big herd of buffaloes was drinking at the pool and a solitary cow elephant came out of the nearby forest. She was screaming her rage for some reason that can only be surmised. Maybe she had lost her calf to a lion or a pack of hyenas. (This is rare but it has been known to happen if the predator succeeds in getting the baby away from both the mother and the rest of the herd for a few moments.) As the elephant approached them all the buffaloes started to rush out of the water, but in such circumstances the last are very much impeded by those in front. The elephant waded in, scooped up the nearest in her outstretched trunk, pulled it onto her long thin tusks, then threw it away dead. It may have weighed very nearly a ton.

It is thought that the elephant, alone amongst mammals other than Man, has a conception of the significance of death. Certainly elephants will return over and over again to the scene of the death of one of their companions and will carry away all the bones and scatter them, and when they have killed a man they will cover the body with brushwood. One night at Treetops, for no apparent reason, a herd of elephants started screaming and rampaging around the building in a manner that defied description. When I went down to the carpark soon after dawn a group was standing in a close circle near the path and I had to tiptoe past them with great care. They were still there when the tourists were due to leave, and that meant taking them out on a distant path and in small groups. After we had all left, and the elephants had gone, the Treetops staff went over to the

Signboard that tells the modern tourist that Treetops is just around the corner. (*Author*)

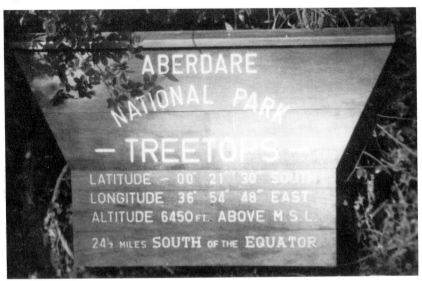

122

place to investigate, and found a newly born calf lying on its side almost dead. When an elephant calves she does so standing up and with a group of her kith and kin standing around as a screen. The calf's drop to the ground is sometimes as much as 6ft (1.8m) and the fall is cushioned by the fluid of the bursting sac. In this case a broken sapling had acted as a spear and the calf had been injured in the head. The chances against this happening must be one in many thousands.

When I returned in the afternoon with another group of tourists the whole herd was back at the site, and the trumpeting went on until well into

Signboard that tells of long ago. *(Author)*

the night. Elephants do not easily forget, and I do not doubt that anyone so unfortunate as to wander near them during their period of communal mourning would have been killed.

When I returned to Treetops in 1978 I quickly noted a family of bush-pigs who used to approach late at night and scrounge for food which had been tossed out of the kitchen windows. According to the records they had been coming for some years, but nobody had taken the trouble to tame them, or to study their habits. The bush-pig is reckoned to be one of the shyer animals in the forest. By sitting on the grass in the area behind the kitchens and tossing them pieces of bread, I brought them to feed out of the hand. It took years and many litters of piglets following one after another, but eventually my Piggie Parties became a feature of Treetops beloved by children and adults alike. Perhaps the most remarkable night came when the matriarchal sow, Gertrude, having fed well, lay on her side whilst a row of tiny piglets suckled and allowed themselves to be stroked. Bush-pigs are striped longitudinally brown and yellow, and are delightful creatures.

Sam was the name I gave to the huge boar, and in those early days I was a little afraid of him. He quickly discovered that if he climbed five steps of the fire-escape to meet me he was assured of more than his share of the pieces of bread. When he heard my footsteps clanging on the iron steps he would run as fast as his short little legs could carry him. The following episode took place during the rains, when children are often allowed at Treetops when we are not full. Katrina Foster was just six years old, and I told her to follow me after dinner, and we would sit together on the sixth step of the fire-escape as Sam could only climb five steps, and that she must give the good pieces of toast to Sam and throw down the burnt pieces to Gertrude and the kids, because if the toast tickled the back of Sam's throat he would climb down again and refuse to participate any longer in the party. This was perfectly true, and had put an end to many a session of pushing pieces of toast between great rubbery lips.

Next morning, down at the Outspan, I was sitting alone at breakfast when Katrina Foster came over to me holding a piece of toast wrapped in a paper serviette, and said: 'When you go back to Treetops tonight give this to Sam. Tell him it is from me. Put plenty of butter on it first and then it won't tickle his throat!' That was not the end of the story. Back in Canada, Katrina started to send me letters regularly, telling me all about her school exams and sports, and at Christmas came a big parcel full of cake with a drawing of Sam and the message, 'For Sam, from Katrina'. Sam did get *some* of that beautiful cake but as he always got a mince-pie from the kitchens on Christmas day I felt he had little to grumble about. Now

Katrina writes to tell me about her dancing lessons. Some day, maybe, it will be to tell me about a boyfriend.

Perhaps the most amusing story concerning the Treetops bush-pigs comes from the night watchman. At 3am a buffalo bull, chased into the pool by a pack of hyenas, aroused the tourists. I heard his voice announcing what had happened but, at that time of night, I was not interested. I have watched many hyena kills and they are not pretty scenes. Usually hyena kill calves or cows but when they are really hungry they will turn on a buffalo bull, and the full pack of around forty animals will wear him down and finally kill him, even if it takes all night. The cacophony of sounds ensured that nobody got any more sleep. One tourist, keen to obtain photographs of the event, came bounding out of his room complete with camera but so deficient in clothes that he had snatched from his bed a blanket and wrapped it tightly around him, holding it in place with his one free hand. His legs and sundry other parts of the anatomy were bare. He was heading for the photographic room, but had obviously never listened to the pleas that the hunter always makes that tourists familiarise themselves with the fire-escapes, for at the first corner he turned right instead of left, ending up on the wrong fire-escape, down which he clattered.

The fire-escape was the one used by the hunter for his Piggie Parties, but the tourist did not know that. He had not been there when I talked about sitting on the sixth step because pigs cannot climb more than five, and so he went right down to the ground. The bush-pigs had eaten quite a good supper from a bowl of sloshy left-overs some hours before, but hope lies eternal in piggie breasts and they were still waiting in the bushes. The camera-toting tourist knew nothing of this. He did not know that a clattering on the fire-escape steps could mean only one thing—that 'seconds' were coming up. Upon hearing the signal the bush-pigs emerged from the shadows, six huge, hairy, black beasts all converging upon one point—the foot of the fire-escape where the now frightened photographer stood, fully convinced that he was destined for the bush-pig menu. He let out a scream far louder than anything uttered by the hyenas enjoying *their* supper, dropped his camera in its new leather case, abandoned his blanket, and shot back up the fire-escape even faster than he had hurried down. And now he made his second navigational error of the night. He turned left instead of carrying straight on, and ended up in the staff sleeping quarters, where terrified waiters thought they were being visited by a ghost.

The night watchman saw all these wonderful happenings from the roof, and hastened down the fire-escape almost as soon as the photographer had vacated it. He retrieved the camera before champing pig jaws could chew up the shiny new leather, and collected the blanket before muddy hooves could trample upon it. Then he hastened to the staff quarters to rescue the 'ghost' before it could be set upon. After calming him down, with some difficulty, he conducted him down the fire-escape which leads to the photographic room, and he duly obtained his pictures.

The crowned crane is a very beautiful bird. It stands 3ft (90cm) tall, wears a golden crown of erect feathers like a halo, and is a mixture of snow white, chocolate brown and powder blue. It is the national emblem of Uganda, a country in which it is much more common than in Kenya. Its haunting cry has been likened to the baying of hounds, but to the superstitious African it is the cry of the tormented souls of long-dead ancestors. They will not touch it for food or in defence of their crops, even though voracious flocks sometimes steal their newly planted maize faster than it it can be put in the ground. A few crowned cranes have always nested in the vicinity of Treetops, but only binoculars have enabled tourists to appreciate their beauty. When Cedric came on the scene he altered all that.

In the spring of that year a couple of crowned cranes nested far out on the grassland and we think hyenas grabbed the female on the eggs, though nobody saw the act. Like swans and geese, crowned cranes mate for life, and soon, in his loneliness, the male, which we called Cedric, wandered close to the lodge. The Egyptian geese were also nesting at that time, and when the goose and the gander proudly brought the line of goslings out of the forest and headed for the Treetops pool Cedric went to meet them. The sight of all those babies aroused in Cedric paternal instincts, and he started to dance. Those who have watched the nuptial dance of the crowned crane will agree that it is a wonderful thing. First the male bows and bobs his head up and down. Then he dances around the object of his devotion jumping higher and higher with wide-spread wings. Cedric did all this, but his emotions were not reciprocated, and the gander chased him away, hissing, whilst the goose hurried her brood into the water, where they could not be followed.

Cedric then turned his attention to the yellow-billed stork, a dour old bachelor who spent most of his time fishing for frogs in the muddy pool and did not want his frogging disturbed. He had a wicked yellow bill and Cedric soon decided that it was not rewarding following him around. Next on the list of possibilities was the grey heron, who was also fishing on the edge of the pond. Cedric pestered him and trailed around after him. He was much bigger than the heron, and so the latter's only means of escape was to fly away and settle on the topmost branch of a tall tree, where Cedric's greater weight prevented him from following. It was amusing watching Cedric settling on thin branches close to the heron, stretching out his great wings as he tried to maintain balance, but failing, and finally having to fly away.

The staff fed Cedric on titbits, and soon he developed the habit of standing by the path at both the visitors' arrival and their departure, and he must have been photographed by thousands of tourists. There was only one casualty, and that was when an overenthusiastic tourist knelt in front of Cedric with a huge lens on his camera, trying to obtain the picture of a lifetime. Cedric saw his own reflection in the lens and gave it a smart peck!

Soon Cedric discovered the baboons hanging around the kitchens waiting for handouts and tried to pal up with them. That was his big mistake. Not only did the baboons not reciprocate but the big dog baboons thought Cedric might be a possible source of food himself and in any event they certainly did not want competition. They had little option about putting up with the wart-hogs but not Cedric. A dominant male baboon finally succeeded in clawing Cedric in the leg and he want lame. We caught Cedric under a sheet and treated his wound but it never really healed, and eventually he just disappeared. All cranes have to run quite a distance before they become airborne. Had the baboons got him I think there would have been tell-tale feathers. Maybe the same hyena that took his wife was the culprit. Cedric was a colourful character, both physically and in his antics, which gave intense pleasure to so many people. We were all sorry when we finally had to admit that we were unlikely ever to see him again.

Baboons have been a mixed blessing at Treetops ever since the early days. They think Treetops was built especially for them, and are so familiar around the place that we have never troubled to count them or include them on the daily lists of animals seen. Sometimes it is a mothers-only day, sometimes it is fathers only, but either way it is always interesting to observe their strict hierarchy—those very low down arrive last on the roof and have to be content with the few crumbs left over from tea. Incidentally, two guards with long sticks are positioned beneath the building to ensure that tea is over, as far as guests are concerned, before the baboons are allowed up.

Mother baboons grooming their babies are always fascinating to watch. They are almost human. The baby is pulled this way and that, and bits of grit and other foreign matter are collected from every crevice exposed. Baboons steal anything and everything, and can open almost every window and door in the building. When they are spotted stealing, the loot can be recovered if one chases fast enough and long enough. They drop it to run just that little bit faster. One day I saw a baboon with something gold and round, which I took to be jewellery. I chased it for nearly a mile in the forest before making it drop the object, which I then discovered was a flat, circular tin of sweets, with tooth holes right through. I wonder if the lady to whom it was eventually returned has that golden tin on her mantel-piece as a souvenir of Treetops. Over the years I have recovered a number of plates of false teeth.

Only once has a guest been bitten so badly that he required stitching in hospital, and that was a huge six-footer who thought he could clip a mis-behaving dog baboon under the ear with the flat of the hand like he would a small boy. Dog baboons have fangs nearly as big as those of a leopard. (There is a record of an adult leopard trying to snatch a baby baboon in the Drakensberg Mountains of South Africa. Two males went to the rescue. One jumped frontally at the leopard, the other landed on its back from behind and killed it with one bite. The one attacking frontally was killed for his bravery.) It is very inadvisable to box the ears of a baboon. Without a moment's hesitation the baboon sank his fangs into the wrist of the foolish tourist, who pulled back violently, ripping the wound wide open. I rushed him to the kitchens, to wash out and disinfect the injury, leaving a heavy blood trail through the dining-room. Then I put on a tourniquet, holding the arm up high, whilst the small vehicle, which always stands in reserve, was brought to the building and a telephone message was sent to the doctor at Nyeri. Only with difficulty was the flow of blood restrained and, half fainting, the man was sat on a chair on the fire-escape to get the cool breeze.

He had a wife and two children, one of whom went hysterical. The wife followed the blood trail into the kitchen, and arrived just as we got him comfortable on the chair. Without a trace of pity she started on him: 'Was it your fault? Tell me now, was it your fault? This could lead to a divorce you know.' By now the vehicle was backing up, and we started to assist him down the winding fire-escape (rather than create a disturbing scene before the rest of the tourists), but she started again: 'You are leaving me without money! I must have some money!' I pleaded with her to let him get on his way down to the hospital, emphasising that the only money she could possibly need at Treetops would be at the bar, and that it would be my honour and privilege to take care of that.

Night came on—and the drinking. I sat her beside me at dinner, and suggested a bottle of wine. She ordered a good white wine, then noticed it was beef and ordered a red, so that both bottles stood side by side—on my account. It is true that hunters at Treetops get a drink allowance, but though I abstained for a month it was still pretty hard on it. At about 10pm the husband was brought back from the hospital with a fist that looked more like a pillow, but at least he could get the other hand into his pocket to keep that avaricious wife going.

I saw that doctor later, and he told me that it had been one of the trickiest jobs he had ever had. It took sixteen stitches to put right a man who thought he could box a baboon's ears and get away with it.

Many years ago, when 'hostesses' were employed, a guest arrived who could only be described as belonging to the opulent society, with jewellery very much in evidence. She was also of the gushing type who never ceased to make a great fuss of me and praised the building and all the wild animals she saw. I suppose I felt unduly flattered and, in a moment of weakness, gave her my visiting card just before she left. Then I forgot all about her.

A few weeks later I came home after a particularly hard three-day duty and went to bed that night feeling I had deserved a good long sleep. About midnight the bedside telephone awoke us with its raucous rattle; in such rare moments it is normal procedure for me to stretch across the recumbent form of my wife and tell the drunken clot at the other end that he has got the wrong number and hang up. This time, however, the voice of the operator was electrifying, for after verifying who I was she said quite clearly: 'Stand by for a call from America.' That brought me out of bed quickly. In fact I was soon kneeling on the carpet in front of the telephone shivering, for I was only wearing my pyjama top.

It was the agitated voice of that wealthy lady, and she quickly came to the point: 'I *must* leave this country. That horrible man Nixon is back in power again. I *must* come and be your hostess. You will meet me at the airport won't you?' Vainly I tried to explain that a foreigner working in Kenya needs a work permit—even for unpaid work—and that such things are extremely difficult to obtain in any Third World country because of the great unemployment amongst its own people. And all the time the sleepy voice of Gertrude Annie insisted that I 'get her off the line and get back into bed'.

'What time is it with you?' went on that unstoppable voice, and when I told her she continued: 'That's funny, its only six o'clock here. I'm up in a twenty-storey flat. I must be your hostess. I'll tell the immigration people that you are my Scottish uncle. You will meet me at the airport won't you?' The agitated voice went on and on, equalled only by the now firm voice of Gertrude Annie demanding I get her off the line. And *I* got colder and colder behind. Eventually I told her I would certainly meet her at the airport—anything for a bit of sleep. I don't know whether she finally settled down—or sobered up—or even if she jumped out of the window.

What I do know is that for weeks I lived in dread that another telephone call would say: 'I'm here—Uncle.'

Sickness is always a possibility at a lodge that caters for so many guests, and one quickly learns to note when there is a doctor in the house, though there is always the possibility of discovering that it is a doctor of philosophy. Over the years I have known of three deaths, though only one occurred whilst I was on duty. Heart problems caused by a combination of age and altitude are the usual cause. It is not often that there is cause for amusement where sickness is concerned but once it did happen.

He was a huge middle-aged man of over 16 stone (100kg) and his wife can only be described as a fussy little shrew. I had discovered there was a doctor 'on board' early in the evening, and so, when I was informed that the big man had had a heart attack in his room, it did not take long to get

Fights to the death in the wild are rare, and rarer still for any man to witness them. In the fifty-four years since Treetops opened it is doubtful if there have been more than a score. This fine water-buck was killed by another the night Her Majesty stayed as a princess, and its mounted head hangs on the wall of the Outspan Hotel lounge. (*Author*)

organised. He was put on oxygen but did not respond and soon the doctor said it was imperative that he be got to hospital, and so the small vehicle was brought from the carpark area to the building.

Carrying a chap of that size down the steep wooden steps of Treetops is not easy, even when there are plenty of volunteers. Space is very limited. The doctor stood at the head of the steps, the fussy little wife by his side. The trouble was that his knuckles were gripping the sides of the stretcher, and there was great risk of knocking them against the rails. The doctor shouted: 'Take his hands off the stretcher and fold his arms over his chest.' The fussy little wife instantly took over, calling: "Enery, 'Enery, do what the doctor tells you; put your arms over your chest.' At this stage I was beginning to wonder whether 'Enery was still alive, let alone capable of carrying out the orders of his loving wife. When we finally got him into the vehicle I thought it was a good opportunity to persuade the wife to travel with him. This she did, all the way to Nairobi, for Nyeri hospital could do no better than us—he had to be got to a lower altitude. But all's well that ends well, and we heard later that he had recovered.

The poaching of elephants for ivory reached its zenith in the mid 1970s. At least one 'plane-load of tusks left Nairobi Airport every week and dhows were loaded regularly at Mombasa. So efficient was the network that ivory from all parts of Africa where elephants could be found was channelled out through Kenya. A lot of politicians in high places became rich, and corruption was rampant down to the lowest level. On two different occasions crates marked 'crockery' fell out of their slings on the Mombasa docks and tusks rolled out. I talked to a dedicated reporter who had vowed that he would clear up the origins of these—but he failed. Today, thank goodness, such wholesale slaughter has been stopped, and elephant numbers are recovering. But the ability to grow really big ivory is genetic. It is doubtful if many 100lb (45kg) elephants will be seen in Kenya in the future.

Forest elephants do not carry big ivory, largely because of the lack of minerals in the soil. They are also bad-tempered, and have an ability to hide in dense cover until the poacher is too close for his health. No large-scale poaching took place on the Aberdares. One of the worst affected areas was Samburu, and the lands to the north. When rhino are persecuted to that extent they simply allow themselves to be exterminated, but not elephants. Something deep inside them, inherited from their remote ancestors, told them that the Aberdares, some 150 miles (240km) away, would give them the refuge for which they craved. There is little doubt that less than fifty years ago migrations between the Aberdares and

Samburu did indeed take place. Today, because of agriculture, miles and miles of stock fencing, and the ditch around so much of the Aberdare National Park, such migrations are almost impossible. About 200 elephants are said to have set off on that long safari. Some were turned back fairly quickly by wardens using aircraft, some stayed on the big ranches around Rumuruti, some were killed by poachers, or game rangers protecting crops and in self-defence, but the majority, thoroughly roused and bad-tempered, reached the National Park boundary.

At that stage it was realised that nothing could turn them back now, neither aircraft nor the thunder-flashes used in game control, and that delay would only result in more deaths, both of farmers and of the elephants. So a stretch of the moat was filled in, liberally sprinkled with elephant dung to give confidence, and the herds were guided over. For about a week the forests around Treetops and the Ark teemed with more elephants than had ever been seen there before. On one night alone I counted 185, coming in herd after herd from the one direction, so that it was easy to tell there had been no duplication of counting.

Not many years after the invasion of the Aberdares by elephants an epidemic of anthrax struck the park. Anthrax has been about the only elephant-killer, other than Man, since the days of the sabre-toothed cats came to an end. The disease is common enough all over Africa amongst cattle, and it might have been brought about by illegal grazing rather than by the elephants moving in. Whatever the cause the most numerous victims were all buffalo bulls, though other animals did succumb, including water-buck, bush-buck and wart-hogs. A strange thing about this die-off was the fact that hyenas would not touch any of the bodies lying around, and vultures only pecked out the eyes, lips and tongue. Packs of hyenas would walk past a dead buffalo and not even look at it. Huge flocks of vultures would descend out of the sky as soon as a buffalo collapsed, gathering round with tremendous noise, fighting and flapping of wings, but none would dare to feed. One vulture lay dead in the morning on the path, and it must be assumed it was the result of unwise feeding. The National Parks authority poured diesel oil over the bodies, and set them afire, but soon they ran out of diesel, and the stench of bodies permeated the air around Treetops.

Going down to the carpark at dawn one morning I found a dead bush-buck on the path, not a nice object for a tourist to have to step around, so I dragged it by the hindlegs and left it hidden behind a bush. Then I started to worry, and read all I could about anthrax, including the facts that cattlemen sometimes get blisters on their hands from milking affected cows, that slaughtermen sometimes get those awful blisters from pushing around affected animals, and that it can finally kill. When I was quite sure the incubation period was past, and I could smile freely again, I asked a veterinary chap amongst the Treetops guests about the precautions I should have taken. 'Oh,' he replied, 'you would have been quite safe if you had put your hands in plastic bags first.' There are hundreds of plastic bags in Treetops used to transport vegetables and fruit.

I suppose all hunters who have worked at Treetops for many years have stories to tell in which they have done something foolish and survived largely due to luck. One hunter of many years told me such a story. He was going down to the carpark at dawn when a terrific noise arose out of the bushes which sounded to him like wart-hogs fighting; so, being curious, he went over to investigate. It was a wart-hog, as he had surmised, but it was not fighting another wart-hog; it was being killed by a leopard, and the path he was walking on led into a cul-de-sac, a little clearing from which the leopard could find no easy line of retreat. In such a situation a leopard is as quick as any animal living. The hunter just had time to lean backwards into the bush and the leopard was past him in a rush. He was lucky it did not slash him as it went.

Not so lucky was a friend of mine in the days when I was a Forester at Kakamega and he was an Agricultural Officer. He was told about a leopard found in a snare by his staff, and he went along with a rifle to shoot it. As he drew near, and before he could fire, the wire snare broke and the leopard was free. He just had time to bend down and the leopard jumped over him, clawing him badly in the back as it went. His name was Dickie Bird but it would appear that when he met a leopard in thick cover, in that final moment of truth, he just couldn't fly fast enough.

Professional hunters faced with the task of having to collect a wounded leopard in dense cover would invariably wear a thick woollen pullover, slacks, a slouch hat pulled down and wellington boots. And they would carry a double-barrel shotgun loaded with buckshot and at the ready.

My own act of folly concerned a rhino, and was brought about by a tourist who looked at my rifle and said in a loud and withering tone: 'I hope that *thing* isn't loaded.' It was an uncalled-for, sarcastic comment, and it hurt. I thought, next time I go down that path I'll carry the two rounds like a professional, between the fingers of the hand; then they can see for themselves it isn't loaded.

A few days after that I left Treetops at dawn and a rhino was standing hidden behind the first blind. He came charging down that earth road in a cloud of dust and puffing like an express train. Two rounds of ammunition between the fingers, an empty gun in the hand! What the hell to do now? All I *could* do was run backwards, desperately trying to open the breach and insert the rounds with fingers that felt as if they were made of wood. Of course he overtook me. I think it was the barrels of the empty rifle pointing at him that made him think I was another rhino, for he slid to a halt just in front of me and jabbed at me repeatedly, making me jump around like the proverbial fairy on a rock-bun. I can remember his little pig-like eyes blinking at me to this day. To cut a long story short I succeeded in loading up just as he decided I wasn't really a rhino after all, and broke off the fight and lumbered away. Never before or since have I been so aware of the beauty of the rounded posterior of a retreating rhino! I felt so weak that I sat down on the nearest log.

The Book of Nature has no beginning and no end, and life is too short to learn more than an infinitely small part of its contents. Even when you think you have mastered the rules, things happen to remind you that there are exceptions; that one should always say that animals *usually* do this or that, never that they *always* do this or that. And, as in the human species, animals from time to time do things that baffle the scientists. Such an event occurred at Treetops even as I tried to finalise this book. I have often thought that the only really successful writers on wildlife are those that deviate from the truth just enough to satisfy a public that craves for the dramatic, but the story of Mom and Bambi, the two water-buck, needs no embellishment. There are times when truth is indeed stranger than fiction. Mom and Bambi lived when others died. Their story has been published in *The Standard,* Kenya's leading daily newspaper (to which I am indebted for permission to reproduce it here).

The drought which affected so much of Kenya in 1984 also affected the game-viewing lodges, and Treetops was no exception. The grass all disappeared, the leaves fell off the trees, and the water in the pool dried up, for the Muringato River was so low that the pump failed to raise it. Many of the animals died; the rest moved up the mountain to where the grass was still green.

The island in the centre of the pool had for many years been covered with papyrus, and some 200 weaver-bird's nests hung suspended from the 20ft (6m) stems. With no water to protect the island, the elephants moved in and, in spite of efforts at driving them away, ate all the papyrus in a few nights, casually spitting out the nests. The birds lost their eggs and their young, for the hyenas ate them by night and the baboons by day. After that the wart-hogs ate the rhizomes (roots), leaving only the bare earth.

The rains came to the ravaged land on 2 October. The island was replanted, and soon the pool filled and new green shoots stood a foot high. The animals all flocked back to a Treetops which was now verdant. On 20 December, at 7pm, a water-buck cow arrived with a calf estimated to be no more than a week old. She took one look at the island, walked up to the water, and jumped in. She swam very slowly, the calf following, with its head resting on the maternal rump. Arriving, she scrambled ashore, and then stood perfectly still, surveying the horizon to make certain she had not been observed.

Papyrus takes two years to reach maturity, and grazing by hungry animals retards growth. Other animals had been out to the island and had been chased away, and a few well-aimed stones had the desired effect in this case also. The water-buck and baby swam back to the shore. The water-buck mother, however, did not run very far; she circled and returned to the pool at a different place, and in ten minutes was again back on the island.

Once before, I had seen a water-buck stare like that before deciding to swim out to the papyrus island. That had been at 3pm on a sunny afternoon and at 4pm she had swum back with a new-born calf. Now I realised that the mother and baby had gone there to escape predators, notably hyenas, and not to search for food. I left them alone, and I gave them names; I called the baby Bambi and the mother Mom.

All that first night Mom lay on the island, with Bambi close beside her. Hour after hour, motionless and with belled ears, she gazed around. At dawn she arose and swam ashore, Bambi dutifully behind her. She had eaten nothing. The next night, at 5pm, Mom again arrived, and again swam out with Bambi. This time she took Bambi to the only bush, in the centre of the island; then, with Bambi virtually invisible except for the very tips of the ears, she swam back alone, and disappeared into the forest. The baby did not follow, and we must assume that some communication had taken place.

Next morning, at 7am, she returned and swam back, allowing Bambi to suckle before they returned to the shore together. On the third night, they arrived together at 6pm, but Mom stayed on the water's edge whilst Bambi swam out alone, and hid under the bush. During the long night Bambi only stood up once or twice, to look around and quickly lie down again. At dawn Mom returned and waited on the shore and in a few moments Bambi stood up and swam across to join her.

With only a few variations in timing the 6pm arrival and 7am departure were a daily routine. Often I would meet Mom wanting to cross the road from the forest as I walked down to the carpark soon after dawn. She never

There are no photographs of Princess Elizabeth at Treetops in 1952 as it was a strictly private visit. This one of a little girl being presented to her in Nairobi is, perhaps, the loveliest of the few available

trusted me, even though I stood quite still, but would go back into the forest and then circle and reach the pool by a different route. Eventually I could recognise Mom and Bambi even though water-buck are so much alike.

On 10 January a big herd of buffalo arrived at the pool just in front of Mom and Bambi to drink, and the milling crowd made Mom very nervous. After half an hour she decided it was not safe amongst such mighty beasts, and she took Bambi back into the forest. It grew quite dark, and I was beginning to think there would be no night spent on the island when suddenly Bambi ran in alone. At the water's edge he did not hesitate but plunged straight in, and was soon out of sight under the bush, for the bush was growing faster than Bambi.

There were nights when hyenas prowled around the pool, and there was a night when a leopard came to drink, but they never suspected that a young antelope was asleep under the bush, and they went away. Both young deer and young antelopes are totally devoid of odour to give them away. Once or twice a big herd of water-buck came to drink just before dawn, and Bambi would stand up, look at them, and then lie down again. One could almost hear him saying: 'My Mom isn't among that lot.'

There came a night when the elephants arrived at the Treetops pool in big numbers, and decided it was bath night. When elephants decide it is bath night they make a carnival of it, rolling, splashing, squirting water over themselves and their friends, and trumpeting loudly. A 7 ton bull submerging himself makes quite a wave; when the whole herd goes in the waves are titanic. Bambi was very frightened. He stood trembling, ran from one end of the island to the other, and almost jumped in. Next night the herd returned, but the only elephant to decide to go into the water was a teenage bull which the matriarchal cow had decided to throw out; in consequence the rest of the herd were ostracising him and so he spent his time alone. Eventually he climbed up onto the island and, as he did so, Bambi stood up and faced him. The surprise was mutual, and Bambi, who had never before seen an elephant so close, was terrified. The bull trumpeted loudly, and spread out his ears. Then he went forward, with small mincing steps, reaching out with his trunk but not daring to touch Bambi. And then he turned around and ran away, entering the water with a tremendous splash, and Bambi eventually lay down again beneath the bush.

Elephants came to Treetops again the following night, at about 10pm, and this time six climbed onto the island. Faced with such a formidable army Bambi jumped up and swam away. I worried about Bambi all next day, wondering if he ever found Mom in a forest so full of night predators, and was greatly relieved when they arrived together just before dark. This time Mom swam across leading Bambi, and never again did she leave him alone.

Now that Mom had decided never again to leave Bambi alone on the island at night because of the unexpected danger from elephants she became more careful than ever not to be seen swimming across, for there was insufficient cover for both of them to hide completely. A baboon barking his warning because a leopard was walking beneath his roosting tree, an Egyptian goose honking his alarm because a hyena was slinking past, and she would stand motionless for a full half-hour before plunging in.

The months following the final disappearance of Mom and Bambi passed quickly, and then, on 25 November, she appeared again at the edge of the pool just before dark, and once more a week-old baby stood at her side. She was a little greyer, perhaps, but again she gave the impression of being a lady of great determination. The baby was even more rufus than Bambi, and the white patches above the hooves showed up more. I gave him the name 'Twinkletoes', not knowing his sex until later.

In spite of attacks by elephants the papyrus on the island had prospered, and was now ten feet tall and still growing, and soon Mom was eyeing it with the same intense stare of 1984. At the water Twinkletoes refused to enter, and eventually Mom pushed him in with her nose, then she herself jumped far out with a huge splash, slowing down so that Twinkletoes could catch up and rest his head on her rump, as Bambi had done.

Heavy rain had fallen all that afternoon, and, upon reaching the island Mom found that she could not climb the soft bank. A smaller island thirty yards away offered an alternative, so she swam there, followed by Twinkletoes. This, however, had little cover, for it was so near the shore we could not protect it. Mom was not happy, and she paced back and forth a long time, finally jumping into the water with Twinkletoes and disappearing into the forest.

Next night, just before dark, Mom and Twinketoes returned, but this time they were accompanied by a fine male, with huge horns. The trio made a fine sight, and there were many comments to that effect from tourists. In both deer and antelopes mothers come into season soon after the birth of the baby, though they may not conceive. The male was purely an opportunist, but Mom was not receptive of his amorous attentions. His chasings, however, drove them apart, presenting any nearby hyena with a golden opportunity of an easy supper. To avoid this Mom plunged into the pool, followed by Twinkletoes and the ardent male in line astern.

Persecution, however, did not cease on the island and soon they were all back and into the forest.

I thought that might be the end of Mom's plans, but I was wrong, for the next night she reappeared, this time without a suitor. In the shallows she could clearly be seen bending over Twinkletoes, and, for just one moment, their noses touched. Immediately Twinkletoes waded in deep, then swam strongly towards the island and hid in the papyrus. Mom watched intently before turning and sauntering into the forest.

The following night three fawns played in the shallows, one being Twinkletoes. Mom stood on the bank but nothing could be seen of the other two mothers. Suddenly Twinkletoes jumped into the water and swam for the island, leaving his puzzled playmates behind. Another night a playmate did follow, but, when left on the mud strip beneath the papyrus he was puzzled what to do next, and eventually swam back alone.

Most evenings Twinkletoes, like Bambi before him, arrived alone, but once Mom came accompanied by another mother and one of the three playmates. Not only did it follow but also hid in the papyrus, whilst both mothers gazed side by side from the shore. Next morning they arrived together and stood until the two youngsters jumped up and swam out. I had visions of a crèche forming but, strange to say, it never happened again. That is not to say it never could, for evolution is slow.

December is the month of migration, when elephants come off the Aberdares and head for Mount Kenya. At least they did before the ditch and its electric fence were installed. Today few make it but still try. Having come from the cold and wet of the high country they do not return but stay and damage trees. In 1985 the migration was heavy. Not only was it heavy but night after night they decided it was bath night, so that life on the island became impossible. Mom started to sleep on the shore with Twinkletoes, moving into the forest when elephants came and swimming across to the island at the first sign of a hyena.

There was one such night when three hyenas suddenly appeared. They were lean bellied and obviously hunting. Both Mom and Twinkletoes jumped into the water and swam strongly, but the hyenas jumped in too, though it was noticeable their speed was slower. In the general panic the two water-buck became separated, Mom on the far side of the island and Twinkletoes on the near. It was then Twinkletoes appeared to become confused, and started to swim in circles, and I was sure he would be grabbed.

At that moment Mom appeared round the corner and swam towards him. What message passed between them we will never know, but immediately Twinkletoes swam to the island and crept into the papyrus. Mom then swam very, very slowly towards the shore, the three hyenas converging behind. Once ashore she galloped away slowly, so slowly I felt certain one of the hyenas would take hold. But Mom's judgement was perfect, and soon she was away and ahead, leading the trio into the night and safe from Twinkletoes.

When the migration ceased Mom again brought Twinkletoes to spend a night on the island. It was early and the island not yet in shadow. Twinkletoes jumped in and headed for the island, but halfway across he changed his mind and returned. Infants are the same the world over! One could imagine him returning to Mom and telling her he wanted to stay just a little longer and play in the sun!

It is now the middle of February, and the weaver birds on the island twitter to themselves, for there is no longer a baby water-buck to be lulled to sleep by their lullaby. Whether there will ever be a third little bambi sleeping there we do not know, for life in the wild is short. Thousands of tourists must have watched the nightly saga of two seasons, but few ever understood. One lady I talked to exclaimed: 'I'm glad you told me it was to escape predators. I was just saying to my friend here—what sort of mother is that to leave her baby behind on the island!'

Scientists tell us that a mother buffalo is bonded to her calf when she nips the umblical cord with her teeth. I am not so sure that other factors are not just as important, such as the first time a calf succeeds in suckling. I became aware of this one night recently when hundreds of buffalo and some thirty elephants came onto the salt-lick at Treetops and many of the buffalo cows had calves or were showing signs of imminent calving. There was a lot of jostling amongst the buffalo, as one expects when so many are competing for salt, and in such circumstances a few calves invariably lose their mothers. One calf, obviously not more than a few hours old as it was still wet and wobbly, went from cow to cow, and even to bulls, trying to suckle, sometimes from the wrong end, but none of the animals appeared interested. Eventually it started to follow a cow that was conspicuous not only because it was heavy with milk but also because it had only half a tail. The cow, however, would not allow it to suckle, moving away every time it tried. This went on for such a long time that it appeared doubtful whether the cow could possibly be the mother. Eventually the proximity of the elephants caused a panic, and in the mix-up the calf got in the way of a young bull, and was tossed aside, the supposed mother making no attempt to interfere.

The calf lay in the mud quite still, and eventually it was thought to be dead. Miraculously, however, it finally stood up and staggered off on another round of trying to find a lost mother. After a while it came to the indifferent cow with only half a tail and, amazingly, it was allowed to suckle. One is forced to the conclusion that only when the mother feels the strain of accumulating milk does she wish to be suckled.

At that stage one of the elephants decided to swim out to the island, and I was obliged to leave the warmth and comfort of the viewing lounge to persuade it to leave. Under Treetops, when large numbers of elephants and buffalo are milling around, one enters an alien world vastly different from the luxury of the place above. Not only is it extremely noisy, with every grunt and snort magnified, but the animals appear twice as big and four times as aggressive. I did not want to spoil the viewing above by 'barking' and driving them all away. My object was to get that one elephant off the island without disturbing the rest.

To achieve this it was necessary to throw stones without revealing one's position, and this meant hiding behind one of the huge pillars supporting the building. Unfortunately some of the buffalo were extremely close, and eventually one of them saw me and started to run; the panic spread like wildfire until every one of that vast multitude was on the move and the elephants screamed their annoyance and formed a huge defensive circle. Did I say *all* of those buffalo ran away? One was left, a tiny calf that had just drunk its first milk. It stood alone in the centre of that circle of screaming elephants. And then a wonderful thing happened—a buffalo cow with only half a tail came galloping through a gap on the far side. Right up to the calf she came, sniffed it briefly, then galloped on, with the calf behind, and both escaped through another gap the elephants made for her as she came near; and I, who stood so near but hidden behind an upright, could only stare and marvel at a mother's bravery. Next night the same herd of buffalo came in, and amongst them was a cow with only half a tail, and a calf that suckled contently.

How ill adapted I was initially to cope with the number of tourists now visiting our game lodges! Like Jim Corbett I was always a loner, with no greater joy than wandering in the forest, and I had to build a shield around myself as a protection against the questions being flung at me continuously.

Dear old ladies can never grasp the fact that a rifle is a necessity at Treetops. 'You don't use *real* bullets do you?' they ask. 'You just put them to sleep, don't you?' Over the years I have evolved a satisfying answer to all questions imaginable. 'No, lady,' I answer, 'we don't put them to sleep. These are real bullets, but we just use them to frighten them away by firing

In February 1969 a fight occurred at Treetops between two bongo bulls on the salt-lick, and it continued until one was eventually killed. Unfortunately hyenas arrived and quickly damaged the skin, so that only the skull and horns could be mounted. The bongo is a beautiful and rare antelope, slightly larger than a water-buck, (bulls have been recorded to 900lb (410kg). At 32in (81cm) the horns of the loser, hanging today in the Treetops lounge, are trophy class. *(Author)*

just over the left ear. We fire over the left ear because it is a little weaker than the right. But you must never be in a hurry. You must always remember the left ear of a charging elephant is always on your right-hand side.' Once I overheard a lady saying to her friend much later: 'I didn't know the left ear of the elephant was weaker than the right.'

The blinds which replaced the obsolete ladders nailed on the trees are, of course, absolutely necessary, especially to staff who are compelled to walk up and down when hunters are not present, yet tourists fail completely to appreciate this fact, even though a huge claim for compensation is at present being made against a tourist firm for the killing of an American lady by a buffalo in 1984. Indeed they very often think the blinds are emergency toilets! People cannot grasp the fact that out of sight is out of mind. I tell them to note the open doorway at either end. When elephants chase them they must run from one to the next, and, when they reach the last, run a bit faster.

The height of stupidity was reached one day when a big herd of elephants was on the salt-lick upon the guests' arrival. We get our guests safely inside when this happens by splitting them into smaller groups, leaving half close to the blind and escorting the others to Treetops by a rather longer but safer route. In the group left behind on this particular day was a beautiful young lady travelling alone and wearing very high heels and a tight skirt. No sooner was I on my way with the first party than she said to all who cared to listen, 'I'm not waiting here,' and off she went, wobbling on those high heels and mincing along in that tight skirt. The staff who push the baggage trolley always remain until last in situations like that. They raced after her, and pushed her none too gently into the nearest blind. Then one of them came to me and told of the predicament, the other remaining on guard. Of course it was imperative that I got my group into Treetops safely before I could return and rescue the young lady from her enforced imprisonment, and by then she was getting more and more indignant. When I finally got her safely up the steps, with the nearest elephant no more than twenty paces away, she turned around, looked down at me and, in a voice intended to brook no argument, said: 'These animals are not really dangerous you know.'

Not all who visit Treetops belong to the lunatic fringe, and sometimes I am thanked appreciatively. I have been given many books by authors, made a Fellow of three zoological societies in three different countries, and taken around in Alaska by a man who said: 'My home will be your home all the time you are in Alaska.' The nicest of all the compliments, however, came from an African tour leader. I have always been a happy-go-lucky person and whistling my joie de vivre has always been a way of expressing my satisfaction with life. One day this man said to me: 'You must have beautiful thoughts—you are always whistling such lovely tunes.'

In finishing this chapter let me repeat the story I told in my book *The African Ark* for it surely belongs in the first rank of comic stories. A little man came plodding behind a huge wife, and the wife was talking as loud and as fast as any wife could. From the viewing lounge could be seen, only a few feet away, a bull elephant placidly munching salt. As the lady came through the door and beheld this magnificent sight, she fell absolutely silent. 'If it only takes an elephant to keep her quiet,' muttered the little man behind, 'then I'll buy a couple off you.'

7
A QUEEN RETURNS

About the time that Eric Sherbrooke Walker was searching the wilds of primitive Uganda and Kenya for his Shangri-La site for a country hotel the author was plodding to an English school five miles each day escorted by two older sisters. In the mind of an eight-year old child the cows in the fields were just as savage as the buffaloes Walker undoubtedly found in the forests of the Aberdares.

Halfway to school, between the Irish Sea and the abruptly-rising massif of Black Combe, one of the outlying mountains of the Lake District, ran a tiny stream no more than a couple of yards across and a foot or so deep. It was well stocked with trout, and the highlight of those daily traipsings to school was watching them dashing upstream or downstream according to where they thought danger lay as the reflection of three little children was cast upon the water.

It is doubtful if many of those trout were more than 6in (15cm) long, but, in a child's mind, they were mighty fish, worthy of being caught by any means possible.

One autumn day a fish lay near the bank that was the grandfather of all the piscatorial members of that stream. Unknown to me the fish was undoubtedly a salmon trout, or sea trout, the name given by scientists to those brown trout that decided years ago to migrate to the sea and acquired the pink flesh and silvery scales of the true salmon through the eating of shrimps. Salmon trout are capable of growing up to 15lb (7kg) in weight, but those that return to fresh water after just six months have usually increased from 6in (15cm) to 12in (30cm), and up to ½lb (250g) in weight. Though such a monster to my juvenile eyes that day, there is little doubt that the fish was indeed a salmon trout, and that it was resting after a run of a few miles from the sea on its way to spawn in the more turbulent water at the stream source in Black Combe a few more miles further on. I

was fascinated and excited as I lay on the bank, my hands outstretched to grasp it.

The moment my inexperienced fingers touched it there was a splash of water in my face and in a moment it had dashed away. Not for many more years were those fingers to become sensitive enough to grasp fish successfully after tickling them in the right places.

Some months later, when again walking along that stream bank, scores and scores of trout were seen lying belly up. A farmer had been dipping his sheep and had allowed the unused, toxic dip, to run into the stream.

That was my first experience of water pollution, a process that was, in the next few decades, to turn many of England's best trout streams into open sewers. That was not the end of the story, for the stream duly recovered when the farmer saw the folly of his action and more trout came up from the sea. Years later I went back to the scene of my childhood and found the stream no more than a trickle, big enough for frogs and minnows only. A holiday resort had been built along that Cumbrian coast, and the water supplying it had been piped from the headwaters of my lovely little stream.

Fortunately Man does sometimes learn from the bitter experiences of others. For me the wheel of fortune did indeed turn full circle during a holiday in Alaska—that last frontier, and the last chance Man has of retaining wilderness on a vast scale—nearly sixty years after the trout stream incident. The Americans are determined to keep that wonderful country just as it was in the beginning of time—untouched, unspoilt, unexploited and undeveloped. A place where Man feels infinitely small and Nature infinitely big.

It was in Katmai National Park, Alaska, that my last salmon was very nearly caught by tickling, and only the sight of monstrous jaws equipped like a shark made me resist from trying.

Brooks River is not big as rivers in Alaska go, maybe 40yds (37m) across and seldom much more than 1yd (1m) deep, so that, with waders, one can fish almost anywhere. It is glacial, gin clear, and with a rocky bed. Only in the fast parts do the fish remain unseen, and they are so numerous that in many places they lie in shoals three deep. Passing over the gravel beds their backs are often half out of the water. In the month of August and in early September the black flies—that scourge of Alaska—are virtually absent.

Queen Elizabeth II and HRH Prince Philip walk across the Treetops Hotel grounds in cheerful mood with park ranger. (*Camerapix*)

Bald eagles will be gathering at that time, forerunners of the legions that will feed on the dead and dying salmon when the spawning is over, sitting on the very tip of the black spruce trees like dolls. Moose will be standing knee-deep in the muskegs just back from the river banks. Bears will be everywhere. And the bears will be catching fish faster and easier than the fishermen.

Brooks River is but four miles (6½km) long and connects two lakes, the larger, Naknek Lake is 240 square miles (640km²) in surface area and has a depth of more than 600ft (185m). There are some who say the finest fishing in the world can be found there as the different species pass through in their season, five species of Pacific salmon, rainbow trout, lake trout, Arctic char, grayling, and other species seldom heard of. At the time of my stay the sockeye salmon were running in their thousands, the best up to 10lbs (4½kg) in weight. Catches up to seventy in a day were by no means unknown, and it was normal practice to return them all other than the odd rainbow trout for the frying pan. Encountering a huge black bear on a blind corner of the river just as a fish was being played I was forced to give him the salmon and take refuge in a black spruce tree on the bank; the only time dangerous animals have made me suffer such an indignity. But in Africa I have always carried a trusty rifle!

There is a saying in Alaska and in Canada that if a bear follows you into a tree it is a black bear. If it tries to shake you out it is a grizzly. If it just sits at the foot of the tree too full of salmon to do anything it is a Kodiak. You see black bears are not always black, and brown bears (of which the grizzly is subspecific), are not always brown. My huge black bear sat at the foot of the tree eating my salmon like a sandwich—he was a Kodiak, the largest of them all because of the salmon he eats.

Before going to Brooks Camp I had sat on a special platform at Portage watching spawning salmon—hundreds of them in shallow water fighting for a place on the redd, or spawning trough. Cock fish would bite lumps out of the tails of other cock-fish.

When I looked at that 10lb (4½kg) sockeye salmon lying in shallow water near the bank of Brooks River, and contemplated emulating the attempt almost sixty years before of tickling a ½lb (250g) salmon trout, I looked at the row of shark-like teeth—and thought of those mutilated fish at Portage.

By the time Her Majesty came back to Treetops on 13 November 1983 not only had I obtained citizenship but I had also become the senior hunter at Treetops. Thus it came about that my path was to meet that of Her Majesty for a brief half-hour and a half-mile of walking together. In this age of technology 500 million people all over the world were to watch, to listen and to wonder.

Although Princess Margaret was unable to visit Treetops during 1956 because the lodge had been burned to the ground, Princess Anne came to Treetops in 1971. (Prince Charles came to Kenya with his sister but he was away camping when she visited Treetops.) It was the night of 11 February and Treetops' 6,544th recorded night of visitors. No elephants were seen but a number of rhino and many of what I like to call our 'bread-and-butter animals'—buffaloes, water-buck, bush-buck, wart-hogs, forest hogs and hyenas. The press were present during the early part of the afternoon but retired to the Outspan before evening so that the rest of her stay could be private.

Just as her mother as a princess had chosen the elderly but famous Jim Corbett to be her escort, so another elderly colonel was to be escort to Princess Anne. Col Eric Adrian Hayes Newington, DSO OBE, known affectionately as 'Hazy' to all his many friends, was another of the Indian Army officers who, like Jim Corbett, left India at the time of Partition and came to Kenya. Eric Hayes Newington, however, did not retire. He joined the Kenya Police and served throughout the Emergency against the Mau Mau, then became a Treetops hunter and did not retire until he was seventy-six. At the time of Princess Anne's visit he was in his seventy-second year. Prince Charles, camping in the Aberdares at this time, and going for long walks in the forest with the warden Bill Woodley as escort, was enjoying himself too much to want to watch animals other than on his two feet.

When Princess Elizabeth, in 1952, had excitedly waved to a small group of people and shouted 'I will come again,' she had no idea it would be so long before she could keep that promise. She had enjoyed what she described as her most thrilling night and was totally unaware that she was no longer a princess but an uncrowned queen. From the moment she was informed of the fact by her husband, in the Royal Lodge, Sagana, she must have realised that she could no longer be a carefree princess, able to wander at will, but must be a monarch, reigning over an empire upon which the sun never set. How well she subsequently ruled, and how deeply she was to be revered by people in what was changing, even then, from Empire to Commonwealth, by a process of evolution beginning in bloodshed but ending in respect, is, perhaps, best illustrated by an incident that occurred along the Airport Road outside Nairobi when she returned to Kenya in November 1983. She was on an official five-day visit, having been invited by Kenya's President Moi during his state visit to Britain some five years earlier.

The welcome the citizens of Kenya gave to Her Majesty that day was remarkable, with every inch of the road from the city centre lined with singing, chanting, flag-waving chilren, and millions of cheering adults of many races, for Kenya today is very much a multi-racial country. The flags of both Kenya and Britain were much in evidence. For hours officials had been going around with huge bundles of them, placing one of each in the hands of the children, regardless of whether they were African, Asian, Arab, Somali or European. It was certainly a day of rejoicing long to be remembered.

Countries which do not have a monarch, and which do not belong to a commonwealth, often fail to grasp the hold those two institutions have over the minds of their people and, failing to understand, are often jealous and try to belittle their significance. A gentleman of that kind stood near as the royal car approached. A little African girl was jumping up and down with a Union Jack in one hand and the Kenya flag in the other, waving them both enthusiastically. The gentleman pointed to the Union Jack and exclaimed: 'What have you got that for? Don't you know they were your colonial masters?' The little girl jumped higher still, and waved her two flags more enthusiastically than ever, and shouted: 'But she's our Queen! She's our Queen!'

First rumours that the Queen might come to Kenya, and possibly to Treetops, came in 1982, and I very nearly cancelled the arrangements I had made for a holiday in Canada. For some years I had been taking my annual leave in different countries, helped by both the National Parks authority and tourists who had been to Treetops and with whom I had kept in touch. By my next leave, in August 1983, it had become much more than a rumour, and the whole of my holiday in Alaska was haunted by the question whether I would be back at Treetops in time for her arrival. Today the world's only really effective answer to international terrorism is never to let the men of violence know just what is happening. Tight security means change, change, change, until the last person in the line feels thoroughly confused. But it also means that he or she cannot talk.

During that famous 1952 visit to Treetops by the young Princess, three rifles had guarded the royal party as it progressed through the forest from carpark to lodge, and early plans at Treetops for the 1983 visit were certainly based upon a repeat of that arrangement. It had also been the system employed for the visit of Queen Elizabeth the Queen Mother in 1959. All reporters briefed in the UK were given a booklet on the Queen's Commonwealth tour and the names of that three-man guard. When, therefore, I was told that I would be one of them I was wildly excited, and felt highly honoured. In fact in my mind I started devising schemes by which I could be nearest to Her Majesty. At that time I imagined the Queen making a private visit devoid of any publicity, just as she had as a princess in 1952, and me walking proudly near her, a member of that three-man guard. How wrong it all proved to be. Not until a short hour before she was due to arrive at Treetops did I learn that I would escort the Queen alone.

When the press came to the Outspan a few days before 13 November, it quickly became obvious to me that they considered I would be playing a major role. In my usual helpful manner I took them on a trip through the Salient, that part of the Aberdare National Park so famous for its concentration of wildlife, and soon they were photographing me against a backdrop of mountains, elephants and buffaloes.

Newspapers in Britain then started publishing pictures on their front pages of the Queen's future 'white hunter'—a term which had not been used in Kenya for quite some years—who would protect her on a history-making return safari to Treetops. I suppose I felt flattered, and I trusted them to report fairly and accurately. Maybe those particular reporters did, but certainly others did not, and things were said in the world media that were quite untrue. Confined as the press were it was impossible for them to hear and see for themselves and so they invented, for they had to provide their readers with a good story. I had, of course, heard of the unfair reporting of the press concerning royalty, but never until they came to Treetops did I actually experience it.

Only those who have been chosen for such high duties as escorting the Queen can have any idea of the fear, the heart-fluttering and the tumult my mind experienced. Would I be ill with 'flu or fever? Would I have a kidney-stone attack, like I suddenly had many years before? Would I have a bad back and be compelled to walk in pain? (That bad back, which comes on every few years, is the result of once trying to eject two big rams from a Forestry Commission plantation in Britain, throwing one animal over the fence whilst pinning the other against the wire with my knees to prevent it escaping, for Lassie, my sheepdog, was small and could not hold them for long.) Or would I just be too dumb with fright to talk?

Plans were still changing day by day as Treetops itself was transformed from a quiet-looking building to one flower-bedecked and 'fit for a queen'. Every step of the various fire-escapes was inspected, and many were replaced. Every beam was checked for strength and white-ant damage. And any cobweb in every remote corner was swept away. The night before the Queen was due there was a big meeting of the company top brass, and I presented them with a list of queries concerning such things as deport-

First sight of Treetops and the ten men waiting in line so patiently to be presented. For a few moments the Queen stops to study them, knowing it is a moment in the history of both Britain and Kenya. (*Paul Roper, Popperfoto*)

ment. Should I be bareheaded in the royal presence? Should I walk on her left side or her right? A foot in front of her or to one side? Should the rifle be carried at the ready, the port or the trail? With tourists I always carry it at the trail. Nice and comfortable, it is true, but it might just point at a toe. All very well with tourists, but with the Queen? Should the breech be open on her arrival to demonstrate safety? Should war medals be worn, even though they might impede movement in an emergency? With tourists I keep the ammunition belt below the jacket and the flap fastened. Precious seconds could be wasted if there were a real emergency, so should it be worn over the jacket and unfastened? In serious hunting one carries two rounds of ammunition between the fingers of the right hand in addition to the loaded rifle. Then how does one shake hands with the Queen? On that conundrum I compromised finally by placing the next two rounds snugly in my right-hand jacket pocket but with the button unfastened. How come the press did not spot that and call it untidy?

The reply to all these queries was short but to the point. They had never, not one of them, walked with a queen in a forest containing dangerous animals, and they did not know. I would just have to think it all out for myself.

The weather in the days preceding 13 November was some of the finest ever known in Nyeri—dreary Nyeri as it is sometimes called because of the mists that are prevalent at that time of the year. In some years Nyeri in November can be very wet and misty indeed. I had asked the powers that be what would happen if it rained, for Kenya rain can sometimes be a deluge. 'Oh,' they cheerfully replied, 'an umbrella will be provided for the Queen, but you, of course, must walk unprotected. You might have to use your rifle, you know.' The October and November short rains, however, had been sufficient to make the land green, and now the sun shone day after day. The jacaranda trees were a mass of mauve blossom, a sight which always gladdens the heart. The flame trees were still a glorious red. And the two Cape chestnut trees which stand just outside Treetops were pinker than I had ever seen them before. One good storm, accompanied by a high wind, would have blown all that lovely blossom away.

As D-day approached I worried about many things, and one of them was how to carry my heavy rifle, a John Wilkes 450/400 double-barrel weapon weighing 11lb (5kg) when loaded. I bought it in 1960 for £70, a fortune at that time, and my wife, Gertrude Annie, was so angry that I promised to finish smoking, a promise I kept. That rifle gave me a lot of trouble in those far-off days, for it double-discharged, a fault which can prove fatal in dealing with dangerous game, but after treatment by an armourer it gave no further problems, and has never failed me since, killing all the 'Big Five' over the years—elephant, rhino, lion, leopard and buffalo. Few people realise that the double-barrelled rifle, which is still used in Africa and Asia, especially in forest areas, represents the peak of British craftsmanship. Handmade, often taking more than a year to produce, usually to the measurements of the client, these rifles are expected to throw to the shoulder with the ease of a shotgun, though weighing twice as much. Sighted to 500yd (450m) they are at their best at close range, where a split second can make the difference between life and death. Science has still not produced a finer rifle in the field of sport, for it cannot jam, being so simple to operate.

Today, ammunition is becoming more and more difficult to obtain, and it will be a sad day for many of the older professional hunters if they ever have to put away their doubles for that reason. I was amazed recently when a visitor from Australia told me that the 450/400 double is still used extensively there for shooting water buffaloes, and that hunters carefully save and reload their empty shells.

Listen to the words of Tony Henley, who was put into hospital for sixteen days after failing to stop a charging lion, though he had hit it in the chest: 'I feel confident that had I been equipped with a heavy double rifle instead of a magazine, I would have got away with it untouched.'

There is inevitably a love-hate relationship between a hunter and his rifle. (This is so even with the doubles, whose sights are fixed and so not adjustable like those of bolt-action guns.) He praises it for his best shots and blames it for his worst, forgetting that it is the operator who really counts.

The 450/400 double was Jim Corbett's favourite when hunting his man-eating tigers in thick jungle, and he mentions it over and over again in his books. After he died in Nyeri in 1955 his rifles were sold in Nairobi, to the same shop where I bought mine. He was, apparently, of my build, and though it is impossible now to trace records, it could well be that I bought one of his rifles. It gives me great pleasure to think that this might be so. Obviously mine has had a great past, for a piece broken from the stock has been replaced with the skill that only a master-craftsman could produce. Apart from its service in the field it has escorted over 100,000 tourists (and one queen) and today must be worth its weight in gold. I am proud of it.

Hunting in dense forests with a sling on a rifle can be very dangerous, and so in the days when I was honorary game warden carrying out control work for the Government, I removed both the sling and its fittings. Now, I thought, they must be found and put back in position. I was searching drawer after drawer when I came upon a small box containing my four war medals, a box not opened again since its arrival. The ribbons were crumpled and the medals tarnished, and it took many moments of nostalgic memory before I could even remember their names. But I did know that the deep blue of the Africa Star must precede the pale blue. The Navy is senior to the RAF. I was to be wearing my medals before a queen whose father had awarded them.

The great day finally dawned and when I found myself with only two more hours to go I decided to spend them amid the bustle of the Outspan Hotel rather than at home, for nerves were fraying. As I left, Gertrude Annie warned: 'Do not have any soup; you will spill it on your uniform.' Even during those last minutes at Treetops there was confusion and change. The senior warden of the park had had a car accident, and, for security reasons, had not been replaced; and when the Provincial warden finally appeared he was in civvies and without a rifle. Only then did I appreciate that I alone would be defending the Queen. Should a buffalo attack, then, in the final moment of truth, it would have to be my rifle and my rifle alone. A ton of moving muscle and blood would have to be stopped by an ounce of lead. It was a sobering thought.

It will, I know, be asked by many whether there really was any danger to the Queen during that walk. No professional hunter will dare to deny the fact that there *was*, and the tusks on the wall of the Treetops lounge, taken from an elephant shot to save a tourist's life, are ample proof. I have seen the Treetops salt-lick covered with nearly 200 elephants, and in such a multitude there are always aggressive mothers with newborn babies, and teenage bulls looking for something to chase, from innocent goslings to baboons and buffaloes. In such an arena I would be loath to venture alone, and would never do so when escorting a Queen. It was for that reason that Nairobi had insisted that fourteen rangers must search around Treetops and chase away any elephants they saw in the forest.

Just how confused people are in their minds about Treetops is illustrated in two extreme views, one from a writer in a popular magazine wishing to sell a million copies, the other from the Chief Constable of a Yorkshire city on looking at my picture on the front page of a daily as he sat at breakfast facing his wife: 'There was no more danger to Her Majesty than she would experience in an afternoon stroll in Hyde Park. The hunter shouted boo to the water-buffalo and the poor thing ran away.' The latter: 'By gum *I* wouldn't like that chap's job tomorrow.' It is quite true that I shout boo to all dangerous animals at Treetops before I fire. But I put a stress on that syllable that makes it sound like a rifle shot. And nine times out of ten it works. And, of course, water-buffaloes do not exist in Kenya.

Finally in position down at the carpark, with the Provincial warden Wilfred Asava on my left, and with the heavy rifle hanging 'broken' over my left arm, we awaited the Queen's arrival. I thought of the many other important people I had escorted into Treetops over the years. In particular I thought of a young princess, the sister of a European monarch. It had been during the commencement of the long rains, and that year the rains had been very late. Treetops had not been full, and the royal party of six had made a great fuss of me. The princess had insisted that I sat in their midst during dinner, and their English was impeccable. She was good-looking and vivacious, and I suppose I myself was not quite as old then. It had rained a little during the night and in the morning the birds sang and

155

the sun shone. It was one of those mornings when the whole world rejoices, making one glad to be alive.

We had walked together slowly, drinking it all in, and when we arrived at the carpark she had suddenly turned to me and said: 'Couldn't you and I walk together in the forest a little further, and let the vehicles pick us up again?' It was a very intriguing thought, and at first I was tempted to agree. Then I thought of the press and the publicity that was bound to follow, especially if a buffalo attacked and had to be shot, and I had to refuse a royal request. I am sure she understood.

It is a steep climb through the forest before the track reaches the Treetops carpark. We heard the vehicles of the royal party stop for a while where there is a small pool, and that meant Her Majesty was late. The press were later to assert that she was late because she was loath to make a return trip to Treetops. We who were there know that it was simply because a big herd of water-buck was drinking and she wanted to stop and watch them. Eventually we heard the two escorting police cars come roaring up the hill. The area of the carpark is small and is encircled on three sides by trees, and there was almost a smash as they skidded into it. I heard the police captain standing on my right mutter 'The —— fools', and instinctively I turned around and, almost before I had time to recover, the royal Range Rover, pennant flying, was beside me, and the Queen was alighting unassisted. A muttered: 'This is your hunter, your Majesty,' and my greatest moment had arrived. I heard myself, in answer to her greeting, saying in a very small voice, 'Thank you, your Majesty'. Instantly HRH The Prince Philip, Duke of Edinburgh, followed with a vigorous hand-shake so different from the touch that protocol dictates for the Queen.

Seconds later, loaded rifle pointing skywards and held firmly by the pistol-grip, I was walking beside Her Majesty, with Wilfred Asava and the Duke following. My mind was in a turmoil. I felt as proud as a strutting turkey, but was aware of the necessity to watch all sides for dangerous animals. Once, as tourists left the carpark, a rhino had come round the first bend like a puffing train, and had only been turned aside by a bullet over the ear accompanied by yelling. I had to guide Her Majesty around the stones and elephant droppings—more than one excited tourist has turned an ankle on the path. And above all I had to listen attentively to all she had to say, though I knew it would not be the foolish prattling of city tourists, who, with an elephant near, so often insist on asking, 'Is that a water-buffalo?' when it is merely a forest hog, and other such inanities. And ever and anon my thoughts went to early army square-bashing days, when 2336901 Signalman Prickett had failed to 'Pull on that butt' sufficient to please a sergeant-major, renowned for a smell of gin as much as a voice heard 200yd (180m) away. Later he had got me on a charge and seven days' confinement to barracks.

Almost at once the Queen commented on the fact that the dirt road, which for years had caused us to bog down during the rains, had been stoned, rolled and watered for 2 miles (3.2km) and under that hot sun had become as smooth as a racetrack. Work had been frantic on it until just before her arrival, and beneath the trees it was still wet. 'You have done it just for me,' she exclaimed, and was assured that, had it not been done, it would have been very dusty. She read the signboard indicating arrival at Treetops, and wondered where the old path could be. She asked me if I had been working at Treetops in 1952, and I had to admit that I had been a British forester at that time. She asked me many questions, and I realised that I was in for a lot more, but under that exquisite charm my natural reserve was fast fading away.

Then we were around the first corner, and it was here I received my first shock, a devastating shock, for a buffalo bull was only thirty paces away on the left, on her side. What were those fourteen rangers doing? I was soon to

The buffalo that refused to get off the salt-lick to make way for the Queen. (*The Nation, Nairobi*)

understand, when I later saw them all standing unarmed beneath a tree. They had pleaded to come back and welcome the Queen, saying that all the elephants had gone away. Suddenly I realised that the buffalo was one of a couple that habitually grazed the glade, and that he was a subordinate. The dominant bull, Satan, was 50yd (45m) further on, and so presented no immediate danger. Yet even this placid one, made subordinate by months of head-bashing, *could* turn nasty. If he did, would I be able to swing the faithful old double as I had done with a huge stock-killing lion in 1962, when engaged on constant government control, putting a right and a left through a heart and a brain? That I could not know, though I had done quite well on the range a few days before. What I *did* know was that, if he did indeed decide to come galloping like a cart-horse, with head up and eyes blazing, the gracious lady beside me would stand like a statue, expecting me to drop him in his tracks.

One camera only had been allowed in the carpark, and the lady carrying it was the cause of my subsequent fears, for she jumped around, pointing its chattering lens everywhere. Slow, steady movement is a necessity when dealing with dangerous animals, and an experience only a few days previously had demonstrated the point. A baboon had succeeded in fishing a lady's handbag out of a bedroom window, in spite of my warning about long hairy arms and the need to keep windows shut. The bag had fallen onto the grass below, the contents spilling in a wide circle. I had seen it happen, and had reached the place before the baboon, although there was a huge bull elephant on the salt-lick, and I had had to walk past him under the building with great care. As I crouched on the grass gathering up the bag and its contents the owner, a young girl, came to the foot of the steps and called out to me, asking if she could come and help. Without thinking I replied yes, forgetting all about that nearby huge bull elephant, and she *ran* to me.

The reaction of that elephant as she ran past him was terrifying. Hitherto he had been scooping up salt and soil with his trunk and transferring it into his mouth. Now he spread his ears and screamed his rage. Fortunately he did not come *under* the building but ran parallel to it, whilst *she* ran back up the steps faster than she had ever run in her life, and *I* hid behind one of the huge pillars of the building.

Pictures subsequently published in the world's press show the buffalo extremely near, me saying something with an obvious air of concern, and the Queen looking back and laughing in great good humour. I will never know, of course, just what I did say, for memory fails when so much was happening all around. What I do know, however, is that when emergencies occur when I am escorting tourists—and they do indeed occur from time to time—and it is essential that I halt the party in order to reassure the animal and to evaluate the situation, I have a habit of exclaiming: 'Hold your hossess!' Sometimes, if the situation is more urgent, I will shout: 'Wahoa, Kate!' Either way the effect on the tourists is to make them stop at once. If I did indeed say that then I hope to goodness it was to that erring and excited photographer, or that at least it was under my breath.

It was during the following moments of evaluating the situation that I instinctively hitched my ammunition belt a little more to the fore of my bush jacket. I have said elsewhere how impossible it was to carry the next rounds of ammunition between the fingers of the right hand, yet it was absolutely essential for me to have unrestricted access to them, and their cool shape under my fingers was reassuring. I had no illusions about the tenacity of life of an enraged buffalo bull. Many years ago, when I was engaged on buffalo control protecting crops for the Government, my pack of dogs brought a wounded bull out of dense cover and right on top of me. That bull took both barrels in the chest fired point-blank and from the hip. He did not flinch but carried on straight over the ground I had stood on a moment before. The dogs held him 30yd (27m) further on, and he collapsed amongst them. When we carved him up we found that his heart was shot into bits. Truly did J. A. Hunter comment in one of his books that the sporting rifle too big for a buffalo has yet to be invented.

My action in pulling the ammunition belt further round, understandable as it was under the circumstances, was to be reflected in the thousands of photographs subsequently published and in television pictures viewed by maybe 500 million people, for my belt buckle was well off-centre, and a crumpled ridge showed right down the jacket front. It is doubtful whether a single person knew the reason why.

The buffalo remained unperturbed as expected, and we proceeded more slowly to the next corner. It was here I had intended to point out to Her Majesty the old rusty nails in an olive tree, all that was left of the original ladders I could remember from my first visit in 1960. But this was the last tree before the straight, and it was too late. The waiting press could now be seen by the Queen. She quickened her steps at once, and the sound of all those motor-driven cameras, the whirring of cinés and the flash of bulbs was perhaps exhilarating to her but to me it was terrifying. What I felt was now something akin to the feeling probably endured by those men in the charge of the Light Brigade. Treetops, in all of its fifty-one years, had never heard the like of it, and I, perforce, had to hurry to keep up with her eager steps, for a Queen was returning, as she had promised she would, when in

1952, not knowing that her father was dead and she no longer a princess, she had called out gaily: 'I will come again.'

Like a man in a dream I moved towards that sea of clicking cameras and flashing bulbs, towards two great flagpoles, one proudly bearing the Union Jack and the other the colours of Kenya. Between them, and under the Union Jack, stood a line of men waiting to be presented: the co-owners of Treetops, Joseph Githenje and James Waibochi, to whom Block Hotels had sold Treetops in 1977, with Block Hotels remaining the management company; and the chairman of Block Hotels, 'Tubby' Block, and his management team of Douglas Francis (financial director), David Stogdale (operations director), Reece Newson (sales and marketing manager), Billy Masoka (general manager of the Outspan/Treetops complex) and Jimmy Masumba (Treetops resident manager). Finally, standing erect but rather nervous amongst all that top company brass, an old Kikuyu man dressed in a resplendent blue uniform. He was Ladislaus Ng'ang'a Njoroge, the cook who had served Her Majesty at Treetops in 1952. His whereabouts had only been discovered a few days previously, in a remote village of mud huts. As soon as the Provincial Commissioner learned about this, he had given orders that Ladislaus must be presented, suitably dressed.

And now it was to be my friend and co-worker's finest hour, for Jimmy Masumba, the next-to-last man in the row to be presented, was to escort the Queen up the steep steps and into the heart of Treetops. We had chaffed Jimmy a lot about this telling him that one must never turn one's back upon royalty, and that he must learn to climb up the steps backwards. Actually, as he told us later, he had no trouble, but climbed 'half and half', pausing every few steps to enquire if she was all right and warning her to be careful of the wooden treads.

The press had drawn lots the previous evening to decide which of the only two positions allocated to them for the Treetops visit each person would go to. These were 'on the ground' and 'on the Treetops roof' and, after setting up their positions before the Queen's arrival in these two places, they were not permitted to move around. No members of the press were allowed actually inside the building, and those taking up their positions on the roof had to remain there during the Queen's arrival below, whilst she was inside Treetops signing the visitors' book and looking at Corbett Corner in the lounge, and after she had left the rooftop for her historic walk to the old site. Not all were happy about this as it would not allow them to hear every word that was said, but they took it in good part and replaced words they could not hear and sights they could not see with the products of their fertile imaginations.

Her Majesty Queen Elizabeth II gallantly attempts to cut the huge welcome back cake until the executive chef arrives to help. (*The Nation, Nairobi*)

Press and television cameras on the rooftop were able to obtain pictures in beautiful sunlight of Her Majesty cutting the magnificent 30lb (14kg) 'welcome back' cake, which turned out to be a daunting task with a small cake knife. Quickly sizing up the situation at the outset, the Duke had said urgently: 'Fetch the chef,' and 'Call the chef, Call the chef,' had echoed along the rooftop from mouth to mouth until it reached Eamon Mullan, Block Hotels chief executive chef, who was in the background, and who immediately sprang forward to assist. Every published photograph shows him, the Queen and Prince Philip laughing over the ridiculous situation of the too-firm icing and the too-fragile knife.

The members of the press on the ground had the advantage of being able to witness much more closely than their colleagues on the rooftop the walk to the old site—and the buffalo. Those on the rooftop could only see it from a lofty distance.

When the last member of the royal party entered Treetops, those members of the press who had been allocated a place on the ground on the other side of the pool surged across the salt-lick like excited children, led by the assistant hunter Paolo Bindi, an experienced man. Paolo is an Italian. Forty-three years ago I was chasing his people out of what was then Abyssinia and Somaliland. But that is now all well into the past. We no longer talk about it, just as there are things I no longer talk about with my Kikuyu fellow-workers at Treetops, whose people, the Mau Mau, burned down the old Treetops two years after the Queen's first visit. I played a part in that fighting too. Thirty years can heal even the hardest of feelings. We are all good friends now and the past is history.

In the general excitement, everybody had forgotten that silent spectator of the Queen's return—the dominant old bull Satan, whose companion had been near us at the beginning of the walk. Throughout the ceremony of the presentation he had stood on the salt-lick glowering, totally oblivious to all the noise, and he had no intention of being driven away to allow the Queen to cross later, or the press photographers to advance now. (I once saw such a buffalo bull argue with a rhino until the blood from constant jabbings of the latter's horn ran down his face.) There were two other bulls further back, but they cleared off immediately, and gave no further trouble. It was a ludicrous situation, but deadly serious—a buffalo bull standing up to an armed hunter and a mob of forty members of the press, each weighed down by cameras and incapable of running. Satan would retreat a few yards, then swing around and stand defiant, once more.

The situation was reaching danger point, and I raced over to assist Paolo. If mayhem was to be avoided, and if a killing had to be done, then it was absolutely essential that the bull went down clean. However, when stones had been thrown he finally took the hint and departed.

By the time I returned to the Treetops building many precious minutes had been lost. Originally it had been planned that I would hurry up the fire-escape and be ready to explain to Her Majesty the Corbett Corner I had created in the Treetops lounge. Jim Corbett is still remembered and revered all over northern India, and I do not doubt for a moment that Her Majesty has never forgotten that he was her final choice of a guest in 1952, or that India honoured him by calling her first National Park after him. I had signed the visitors' book in his old home, and had a lot to tell her. A voice was calling: 'Mr Prickett is wanted upstairs,' but I knew it was too late, for already I could see the royal party returning to the steps. Once again well-laid plans had gone awry.

As I joined the Queen and the Duke to escort them over to the site of the old Treetops, I again took my place on her right-hand side, trying to keep her eager steps in check and away from the worst of the rough ground. She

Sitting in 'Corbett's Corner', and flanked by the owners Waibochi and Githenje, Her Majesty Queen Elizabeth II signs the visitor's book at Treetops, whilst Prince Philip looks at the photographs. What poignant memories this must have brought back of 1952!

appeared to be wanting to find the path of yesteryear, and kept heading towards the distant forest instead of around the pool and towards the old site as planned. Elephant droppings, stones and stumps were scattered everywhere, but she detected them and trod lightly, and had little need of my guiding hand. Of course she was concerned about the retreat of the forest, and we discussed ways of arresting it at some length, but she also knew that the population of Kenya has more than trebled since 1952, that the tropical rain-forests of the world are but a pitiful remnant of their former splendour, that nearly half a million people have rejoiced seeing the overabundance of animals around Treetops, and that these factors had made environmental change inevitable. I told her many people were concerned, and that plans were afoot to arrest the retreat.

Wart-hogs, bush-buck and baboons were everywhere, and each group we encountered drew admiring comments from the Queen. The baboons had been absent, raiding the crops of the local farmers across the boundary ditch in spite of its electric fence. Today they were present in strength, having forgotten the ripening maize. She asked me about those buffalo bulls, and I described them as just retired old gentlemen. This amused her greatly, and she passed my answer to the Duke, who was walking much nearer the water with Wilfred Asava, calling back; 'Philip, Philip, he says it is all right, they are just retired old gentlemen.' I had noted every stone beforehand, and soon we were on the spot indicated by the press for perfect photography.

The press were lined up with Paolo Bindi behind a thick white rope some thirty paces further on. They had carefully measured the distance the day before, and placed a tiny twig on the ground. Here I halted, and pointed to the new Treetops across the water, and the gesture drew a barrage from those clicking cameras. Then we arrived at the site of the old Treetops, and I suddenly became aware that the dominant old bull, Satan, though driven off the salt-lick to make way for the Queen, had not left the area but stood facing us some 50yd (45m) further on. With Paolo Bindi now so near me, I knew that between us we had sufficient fire-power for any emergency. I pointed Satan out to Her Majesty, and Queen and buffalo stared at each other for a long, long minute.

And then a strange thing happened. Satan, who had been resolutely staring at the Queen, suddenly started walking *towards* us, and just as I was beginning nervously to grip the rifle, he stopped at what was now little more than twenty paces away. Then an even more wondrous thing happened; he started to kneel down facing Her Majesty, with hindquarters high in the air, and I remember muttering, with suspended breath: 'He's going to lie down.' The next moment he threw himself sideways, still facing us. I know that buffalo always lie that way, but to me that kneeling down was an act of supplication to the Queen, and maybe his apology for being so rude as to keep her waiting on the salt-lick.

The Queen turned abruptly and I walked over with her to the stones, pointing out the concrete blocks that were mute reminders of the 1954 fire which destroyed the building and much of the fig-tree. Those blocks had been necessary as a base for the poles which steadied the tree, for two extra rooms had had to be added to accommodate the 1952 royal party, and each block had an 8in (200mm) hole in the centre. All this I explained to her whilst she stood in silence, deep in her own thoughts. I do not think she grieved, though she had loved her father so dearly. But thirty-one years, almost thirty-two, was in 1983 a little more than half her lifetime. The press did not have to twist events to their own conclusions. Finally the Queen turned away and we headed back to the new Treetops.

It was now that the full significance of this historic event suddenly struck me. Over a hundred elephants had stood on and around the salt-lick at

7.30am that very morning, and Paolo Bindi had had great difficulty getting all the tourists out safely, finally having to use the big bus. In that mighty throng, the biggest that rainy season, there *must* have been some elephants who were present in 1952, and who without those fourteen rangers patrolling would undoubtedly have returned. Even as I thought these thoughts a big herd of those regal antelopes, the water-buck, was trooping down to drink and I pointed them out to the Queen.

On our return walk across the glade the Queen brightened, and we talked of many things. I found myself telling her about Tiger Tops, in Nepal, and the many wonderful animals I had seen there; of Alaska and its bears, and how, when salmon-fishing a small river, I had been confronted in midstream at a bend by a huge Brownie, the very grandfather of all Alaskan brown bears, and how I had been compelled to climb a tree to save my fish. The account of my undignified ascent amused her. I will remember that genuine laugh as long as I live. Then she suddenly stopped, and said that she had only seen those animals in zoos. It struck me forcibly that I, a mere commoner, with limited financial resources, could see them whenever I wished. I had wings, whilst she, monarch of a nation of 60 million people, and head of a Commonwealth of 1,000 million more, had to bow to protocol. I am sure she enjoyed those few minutes ahead on our own, away from the press and even from the Duke and Asava, and away, even if only for such a brief spell, from the pomp and splendour surrounding her normal life.

All too soon we reached the carpark and my finest hour was over. But before this happened something occurred which emphasised the Queen's unfailing charm. As we joined the hard path the remainder of the royal party, press, security people and the Block Hotels top brass came surging behind. As we actually reached the vehicles I dropped back amongst them, for my mission was now over. For a few paces the Queen carried on, then she turned back, threaded her way through the throng, smiled at me, shook hands, and thanked me before bidding me farewell. Amidst frantic waving the last vehicle went down the hill and suddenly the carpark was empty. They were gone.

Slowly I turned and walked back to Treetops alone, on a path I must have travelled 10,000 times but only once with a queen. I felt lonely and very thirsty, and my left shoulder ached with the weight of the rifle. Reaching Treetops I drank at least six cups of tea. By then it was time to return and meet the tourists coming in, for it had proved impossible to turn them all away, though the Central Reservations Department of Block Hotels had tried very hard. I was walking deep in thought along the path, and the bull elephant caught me out behind the last blind—a huge bull that should never have been there. He blew noisily down his trunk as he stood facing me no more than a dozen paces away. Two quick strides followed by a flailing trunk and he could have flattened me. But he didn't. He just turned and shambled away. Was he laughing to himself because he had thwarted the efforts of fourteen rangers?

I was taking care of the seventeen tourists later that evening when the telephone rang. The telephone line to Treetops goes underground for the last mile and, because of this, reception is often poor. It was a news reporter, calling from Glasgow in Scotland, and he said he had a woman by his side. Through the crackling he tried to explain to me that she had seen my photo in the British press and was sure I was her long-lost father, who had married in 1943, later divorced, and had been called Richard Prickett. She had his photograph beside her. Through the babble I could hear her voice calling: 'It's Rosemary, Rosemary, Rosemary.' The call came again later in the evening, when reception was much better. And when I finally convinced her it could not possibly be me I could hear the sob in her voice. I could only console her by promising to answer her letters and help trace her father in any way I could.

Returning to the Outspan from Treetops the next morning at 8am I could not face breakfast and decided to go straight home to Gertrude Annie. Once in the quiet of the bedroom tensions eased, and the tears began to well unashamedly, whilst a wife who has played the waiting game for more than forty years, through war and through peace, consoled and comforted me.

Next day the wonderful weather we had been experiencing for so long broke, and violent storms swept across the Aberdares and Mount Kenya. The day after that, when I was leading a full house into Treetops along that famous path, there was suddenly a loud scream behind me. I thought of those two tourists recently killed by buffaloes at another Kenya lodge, and I turned, fearing the worst. Instead of a rampaging buffalo a young girl in open-fronted sandals stood more than ankle deep in an elephant pat that would have filled a wheelbarrow. I smiled. Treetops was fast getting back to normal.

Five weeks after the Queen trod the Treetops path Satan was shot by Paolo Bindi as he escorted the lady housekeeper at dawn. That dawn trip to the carpark to check vehicles, and the return trip with relief staff, has been a Treetops routine for more than half a century, with only a short gap after the original Treetops was burned down. On most mornings it is uneventful if cold, but sooner or later an incident occurs. I do not doubt wild animals recognise and evaluate people just as thoroughly as we do them. Certainly Satan appeared to hate Bindi. He would come galloping up with head held high and a peculiar wild glint in his eyes. Then he would circle. At twenty paces this usually resulted in a shot being fired as close to his head as possible, for the screaming bullet adds greatly to the power of intimidation. This happened on that fateful morning and Satan sheered away as usual. Then he changed his mind and came back in a full-blooded charge.

I am glad it was Paolo and not me who had to shoot Satan. Once, I could kill with the cold precision of the professional; indeed, my finest shots have always been when endangered. But that was when I was young, and the inherited blood of my hunter ancestors coursed hot. Now I have watched these animals just a little too long, a little too closely, and a little too near.

8

RETREAT OF THE FOREST

'What have you done with all the trees?' When the owner of Treetops was asked that question by Her Majesty, and had only seconds in which to answer, his reply, 'The elephants have eaten them all Your Majesty,' was the only possible one. But how unfair it was to blame the elephants for the whole problem. Out of the 26,000 tourists estimated to visit Treetops every year, many have asked that same question. Some have even gone as far as to assert that all the dead and dying trees should be removed in order to tidy up the forest, as though Nature had any use for the words 'tidy' and 'untidy'. The writer has been a forester for twenty-two years, and has been involved with wildlife for many more, but he still does not know the answers to many complex questions. However, when the reader has come to the end of this chapter, he or she will surely know some of the reasons for the retreat of the forests in the vicinity of Treetops.

'The forests do not hold a lot of wild animals.' Those words were said to me by an old Kenya settler who had carved his farm out of the virgin montane rain-forests in the early days of the century. The date was October 1941, and I was enjoying my first army leave at the end of the Abyssinian campaign. I had spent the whole day trout fishing in the forest, and I suppose I had grumbled, for the animals I had seen could be counted on the fingers of one hand. Over the years I did better. Nevertheless it was a long time before I could say I had seen all that the forests had to offer. Today, a tourist can see more from any of Kenya's forest lodges, and the viewing will be in comfort, with a glass of beer to hand, not on hands and knees and crouched behind bushes, as I had to do it.

It must be remembered, however, that the forests that old settler was referring to, and the ones I had been fishing and hunting in, were 'in balance', with a closed canopy overhead. A price has been paid, and is still being paid, for the wonderful viewing from our forest lodges—Treetops,

On the dining room wall at Treetops are the tusks of a cow elephant, surrounded by photographs depicting the incident, which was shot on 7 May 1968 to save the life of an Australian tourist. The baby of the elephant was stuck in the mud and she was frantic with anxiety, blaming all who approached for her troubles. After the death the herd returned, and rescued the calf. A calf can suckle any elephant mother. (*Author*)

the Ark, Mountain Lodge and the now defunct Secret Valley.

The Royal Aberdare National Park does not contain a lot of wildlife and must primarily be considered of botanical interest only. Those words, or words to that effect, were incorporated in a report made in 1959 apropos the handing over to the National Parks authority of a huge area (approximately 300 square miles / 800km²) of forest estate belonging to the Forest Department, and destined to become the present-day Aberdare National Park. I was at Kiandongoro Forest Station, and to the best of my knowledge that report still lies mouldering in the pigeon-hole to which I returned the file.

A perfect forest is a botanical wilderness. Those words, written by a scientist, refer to the dense conifer forests of the northern hemisphere, where the 'botanical wilderness' can sometimes be so intense that there is nothing but needles on the forest floor, but the description is just as applicable to some of our tropical rain-forests, and especially to that wide belt of Alpine bamboo that girdles all our mountains between 9,000ft (2,750m) and 10,000ft (3,050m).

If the forests of Kenya never produce anything other than water they will still

169

show a profit. Those words can be found written into the Annual Report of the Kenya Forest Department by the Chief Conservator of Forests in 1957. He was not referring to the vast plantations of pine and cypress that were being established even then to meet the needs of an ever-expanding human population, nor yet to National Parks as yet unborn, but to the vast areas of virgin forest covering so much of Kenya at that time. Cypress and pine are a poor substitute, as regards retaining water, for the indigenous forests, and it is a pity more people did not heed his words.

Treetops was the first game-viewing lodge to be built in Kenya, and possibly in the world. It opened on 6 November 1932. In the fifty-three years since then a lot has happened. Whether a lot has been learned remains to be seen.

I have already explained how, in 1932, Treetops was built in a Forest Reserve under an administration that only then gazetted the forest, thus making its boundaries legal. It was never deep within the forest, but close to the boundaries of the farms that had been allocated to soldier-settlers, and so it was affected by the adverse activities of a national population that was estimated at only 3 million in 1932 but had risen to nearly 20 million by 1985. Until the gazettement of the National Park in 1950 (and for many years after, because of Mau Mau), Treetops and its vicinity were subjected to illegal grazing, firewood collecting, honey and meat hunting and a slight degree of illegal cultivation.

Let me describe three incidents demonstrating the threat posed by these factors. The first occurred many years ago, before the digging of the moat on the eastern perimeter of the Park. A retired Indian Army colonel was the hunter-escort and, being a heavy drinker, liked nothing better than serving at the bar himself, with his own bottle of whisky beneath the counter. One afternoon a tourist came up and said: 'Colonel, there's a herd of cows drinking at the pool.' 'Oh no,' said the Colonel, in his best 'straight from Poona' voice. 'Those are not cows; they are buffaloes.' When three different tourists had come up with the same comment he thought it was time to come round from the bar and investigate. They were cows.

On another afternoon, much later, I was on duty when I spotted through binoculars a group of people in the distance. Jumping into the stand-by vehicle I went straight down to the National Parks authority headquarters and collected a ranger, and together we went out to investigate. We found a dozen women, each with a huge load of firewood, and we took them to the police. They were eventually fined 100 shillings each, a considerable sum of money at that time.

On another occasion a group of young men, each carrying a long stick, could be seen in the far distance. At first we could not ascertain what they were doing, but later discovered they were chasing wart-hog piglets, of which there were many at that time of year. We 'phoned the National Parks authority and in less than fifteen minutes a plane was circling over the area, and an effective stop was put to piggie chasing. Had a helicopter been available I do not doubt an arrest could have been made.

These are examples of just three factors that have contributed to the ultimate retreat of the forest. There are many more. A herd of cattle getting into the forest, a few women gathering firewood from fallen trees, a group of hungry youths having fun chasing piglets may all sound innocent and of course on a small scale can be innocent. But for every case discovered it can be assumed a hundred more go undetected.

'I do not like elephants; they destroy all the trees.' How many times have tourists said that—or words to that effect—to me! Invariably, when I have chatted to them about the role of the elephant in Nature's grand scheme of things, they have admitted that they never thought of the elephant in that way. Elephants, of various species, have inhabited all the continents of both the New and Old Worlds with the possible exception of Australia. Just as the Siberian tiger has been the very apex of the carnivores ever since the disappearance of the sabre-toothed cats, so has the elephant been the very apex of the herbivores. All lesser creatures, and this has included Man himself, have been subservient to them, and have depended on them for their very existence.

Without Man's interference, all areas of the earth's surface, wherever the soil and climate are right, end up under a blanket of forest, a fact well illustrated in John Still's book *The Jungle Tide*. In Nature there are no such things as axes and saws, fire only occurs by lightning or volcanic action, and disease is almost unknown when forests are 'in balance'. And so it becomes necessary for Nature to operate a 'conversion factor'—something to convert unpalatable high forest, fit only for monkeys, birds and butterflies, into bush and grass, suitable for a host of lesser creatures. And that is the role of the elephant. When I explain this to the tourists they invariably admit that they have never thought of the elephant in that capacity.

Elephants, however, have other roles to play in Nature's grand scheme of things besides being 'conversion factors'. They are the world's finest road builders. They grade their roads with such engineering skill that most of Kenya's orginal roads were based on elephant trails. And once a road has been made by elephants it is used by every other denizen of the forest, from the diminutive suni (tiny antelope) to the ponderous rhino. In a tropical rain-forest where the elephants have been exterminated it is extremely

171

difficult and expensive to move around. I know this, having worked in them. Besides being first-class road engineers elephants are great protectors against soil erosion, both in the forests and in the dry country. As they walk their well-aligned roads they continually pull down foliage and feed, and as they feed small pieces continually fall onto the path and are trodden into the soil. And when herds of 100 elephants tread these branches, walking in Indian fashion, they create a wonderful road that will never become eroded.

In dry areas elephants often roll in favoured places until they have completely coated themselves with mud. Their great weight compacts the soil and such a place becomes watertight, providing small animals unable to migrate with water long after the rest of the land is dry. Elephants do not digest all of the vast quantity of foliage they eat, and the seeds of many plants pass through unharmed. The great mass of coarse-fibred droppings, sufficient to fill a wheelbarrow per elephant, provides a perfect medium for growth in dry places. Practically every Borassus palm-tree in Uganda has grown from a seed that has first passed through the stomach of an elephant. And when an elephant dies, and 7 tons rots back into the soil, an area of about $\frac{1}{2}$ acre (2,000m^2) benefits.

In the days before Man's proliferation prevented the use of elephant trails, and cultivation destroyed many more, elephants travelled between all the mountains, to all the rivers, and to the most remote drinking holes. And they did not respect international boundaries. They could, and often did, migrate hundreds of miles to obtain salts and minerals, or to eat rare plants. It is doubtful whether there is any place left in Africa where elephants can now wander and acquire all that the body yearns for, not even in that largest of all African National Parks, the Kruger. And the areas they are allowed to wander in unmolested get smaller year by year. The result of all this is that they visit favoured localities far too often. When I was a forester on both Mount Kenya and the Aberdares, months would sometimes pass before elephants returned to the parts in which I hunted. There was one stretch of the Chania River where I fished which had, in the vicinity, many wild banana trees. The elephants returned every year, just as the small fruit was ripening.

Young bull elephants, like young schoolboys, love to try out their strength pushing over trees, and isolated trees become a prime target. Some National Parks have made a habit of shooting such animals. It is wrong, of course, for if man had not interfered in the first place, such excesses would not be so harmful and could be forgiven.

Whether a National Park is overstocked with elephants is difficult to

The baby elephant born at Treetops outside the kitchens during the night of 7 July 1982, and whose subsequent death caused so much consternation in the herd. *(Block Hotels Archives)*

decide. In forest areas it is not easy to know the population, for aerial photography, so successful on the plains, is of little help. In a forest environment only a dedicated warden, flying over the Park himself and studying the reports of every patrol, can have any idea of the true figures. We know that forest elephants, because of the small ivory that they carry, are not subject to the same degree of poaching. We know that National Parks are always loath to admit that they have too many animals of any species. We know that some tourists would not be satisfied even if elephants walked around them all day long. And we know that when Man the hunter ceases to hunt, elephants invariably increase because they have no other efficient predator. The chances are that most of our National Parks are overstocked, in spite of the poaching problem.

A hunter-escort at Treetops is sometimes almost driven insane by that everlasting question: 'What time are the elephants coming in?' One night, at dinner, a disgruntled tourist made quite a scene because no elephants had been seen, demanding his money back. So objectionable was he that eventually another tourist shouted: 'Why don't you go to a zoo?'

Treetops is situated on an old elephant migration trail linking the Aberdares and Mount Kenya. Before the moat was dug to protect the intensive cultivation, elephants migrated between the two mountain masses every rainy season, and must have done so for thousands of years. It is doubtful, however, if they stayed many days before moving on. Today the urge to migrate is still there, and they still arrive, but the moat, especially since the electric fence was installed on the top, effectively stops them. They are then frustrated and hang around the area a long time before returning. They do not return, however, to the bamboo zone and the moorlands—it is far too cold and wet there, and they hate dripping water on their backs. They move into the foothills. That is why a retreat of the forest is evident far from Treetops.

Having looked at the role of the elephant in Nature, and seen that, though the elephant has contributed to it, the retreat of the forest has been brought about by the irresponsible behaviour of Man, let us now turn to the predators of the Aberdares.

Scientists tell us that the Pleistocene epoch came to an end 10,000 years ago, and with it the last of the sabre-toothed cats—a group of felines with huge fangs capable of tackling the mammoth, the woolly rhinoceros and the mastodons, and later the forebear of our modern hairless elephant, *Elephas antiquus*. Few scientists, however, mention that there is still one relic of the sabre-toothed cats with us—the now endangered clouded leopard of Asia, smaller than the common leopard yet with huge fangs capable of killing the sambur, a deer larger than the European red deer.

During the Pleistocene epoch the Afro-Alpine climate we find today on the moorlands of the Aberdares reached to the plains between Mount Kenya and the Aberdares, and the climate above must have been too harsh for an abundance of wildlife. As the climate improved, animals from the low country would be found migrating upwards through the forests and finally onto the moorlands. Proof of this comes from the fossil bones of a species of bongo very similar to that of the Eastern bongo we find today on the Aberdares; these bones are found in the Omo deposits north of Lake Turkana, many hundreds of miles away. Eland, zebra and lions following them have been a feature of much more recent times, resulting from over-hunting by Man. When this colonisation from the low country took place, there was a lack of adequate predators, but this role has been taken by Man and recently by hyena.

There was, however, one likely predator of the high country of both Mount Kenya and the Aberdares, and in the early 1930s a man spent years trying to prove it existed. He was Kenneth Gandar Dower, and his book *The Spotted Lion* makes fascinating reading. Two skins of a fantastically spotted animal were obtained, with a jumble of bones that might or might not have belonged to them. The trouble was the sportsmen who shot those lions left the bones behind, and hyenas scattered what they did not eat. Under those circumstances scientists would not accept the evidence of a new subspecies. However, local Africans knew the animal well, and had a name for it—*marozi*. A number of sightings of the animal were also made by reliable European sportsmen.

All lions originated in a forest environment, and the spots on the stomach of virtually all cubs prove it. In addition to lions moving up from the plains, a number of lions trapped for the crime of cattle-killing have been released on the moorlands in recent years to boost the numbers of predators. Inter-breeding would thus have taken place with any *marozis* and so now we shall never know if such an animal really existed.

Whether it was wise to release stock-killing lions onto the cold moorlands, even though a shortage of predators undoubtedly existed, is a debatable point. During the year following that of the Queen's return to Treetops, a lion mauled and almost killed a Swedish lady at a famous beauty spot in the Aberdare National Park on a road opened by the Queen Mother in 1959. The altitude was around 10,000ft (3,050m). Camping had been banned in the area for some time, following an incident where a lion had slashed open a tent during the night. Fortunately the lion failed to grab the occupant, who escaped to his vehicle. There had followed numerous incidents of picnickers suddenly discovering they were being stalked by a lion and fleeing to their cars, and warning notices had subsequently been erected.

On the morning of the near-tragedy, three people arrived—a woman with her child and husband. They parked their Land-rover, and whilst the husband stayed a few moments behind to attend to it the woman, carrying the child, proceeded down a path leading to the falls for which the place is famous. A big male lion reared out of the grass, and she had the presence of mind to throw the child from her and cover her neck with her arms as a protection before she was knocked to the ground. The lion carried her away, presumably as a prelude to eating her. Upon hearing her shouts the husband followed in the vehicle and succeeded in making the beast drop its prey. After a long delay the Flying Doctors Service arrived and took the victim to a Nairobi hospital, where she lay on the danger list for a week. The lion was never accounted for, though the hunt went on for a long time. It is not unreasonable to suppose that it was one that had failed to acclimatise to the cold, or had failed in hunting a new species of prey in a new type of habitat in competition with other lions.

There are some who scoff at the idea that there is anything left for science to discover, claiming that the yeti, the Loch Ness Monster, the Nandi bear and the *marozi* are figments of the imagination. I do not agree. I believe that mammals, birds and reptiles have become extinct even in this twentieth century, before science had a chance to study them properly. Some of them may have died out just because their evolutionary span had come to an end, or because the world no longer supplied their requirements. The fossil record, wonderful though it is, does not give a complete picture of the creatures that have lived on this earth, and fossils on both Mount Kenya and the Aberdares are conspicuous by their absence. There is evidence that in the depths of the ocean there are creatures even more awesome than any seen on dry land: a shark's tooth, many times bigger than any shark known to science, caught in a fisherman's net; shadowy forms of huge proportions following in the wake of boats and seen by captains of unquestionable integrity. It could well be that on Mount Kenya and the Aberdares the major predator between the demise of the sabre-toothed cats at the end of the Pleistocene epoch and the arrival of the Gumba and the Wandorobo hunter-gatherers was indeed the *marozi*.

Turning away from the subject of what animals kept the balance of nature until recent times we come to the problems that arise when that balance is upset. Science calls the weight of animals on any given area of land its biomass. The biomass of animals in the vicinity of Treetops has, over the years, increased until the land can no longer support the biomass as forest. Now let us see what happens when that point is reached.

Underneath the canopy formed by the big trees of montane rain-forests is a dense understorey, some of which is a generation of the trees themselves but much of which is bush, interlaced with creepers and vines. Much of this 'bush' is *Sambucus* and *Crotalaria,* but exactly what the bush consists of does not concern us here; what concerns us is what happens when the feet of too many elephants, rhino, buffalo and other animals trample it out of existence, to be ultimately replaced by grass. Forest trees have grown in association with this bush since they were saplings, and there is an interdependence of the root systems that is still imperfectly understood by scientists.

The soil contains mycorrhiza—a non-pathogenic (non-disease-producing) association of a fungus with a vascular plant (brophyte), to the mutual benefit of both. Without mycorrhiza certain trees cannot grow satisfactorily. During the early days of this century the Forest Department in Kenya decided to grow pines as a substitute for the slow-growing indigenous hardwoods, as a source of building timber and as pulpwood for the paper industry. They imported the seed and planted it according to the rules of good nursery practice. Nowhere in the country would the seedlings grow. The seeds germinated, grew a few inches, then faded away. It was years before a silviculturist decided to import pine soil from the place of origin of the seed—South Africa. The results were remarkable. Not only did the seedlings grow but the trees themselves came to make an important contribution to the economy of the country. From that moment it became standard practice to import pine soil into the nursery, first from South Africa and later from older plantations, for the local soil did not contain the necessary mycorrhiza.

In all of Kenya's montane rain-forests a few trees will be seen to be stag-headed as a result of old age, but when the biomass is too high the number of stag-headed trees suddenly increases. The topmost shoot of the tree dies and then others follow. Down in the soil, however, other things are taking place. The root tips are also dying, and when the tree finally falls, sometimes years later, only a bunch the size and shape of a barrel will remain. Wind, sun, rain and the trampling of too many feet have battered the crumb structure of the soil until it has become like cement, so that roots cannot penetrate it or find sustenance in it. During the rains, when for a short time the soil becomes soft, these isolated trees will go crashing down like nine-pins. They also become a temptation to any of the big game animals, to push them over. When tourists watch such a tree being pushed down by an elephant they are not aware that its root system has already gone.

An interesting example of how some trees can survive when others have died all around them is the group of three pearwood trees and two Cape chestnut that grow around Treetops itself. One of them, a huge pearwood, grows right through the middle of the building and 20ft (6m) above the roof. Here, the building provides them with shade for more than half the day, and the proximity of staff ensures that what Adraan Kortlandt calls the 'bulldozer herbivores' keep their distance, and so do not compact the soil. During the great drought of 1984 the trees had to be watered, and it will be a sad day for the image of Treetops when they die, as die ultimately they will. Figs and olives are amongst the trees prone to sun-scorch when robbed of the shade formerly provided by their associates. The bark may split longitudinally or they may simply start to become stag-headed.

The Kakamega forest, in Western Kenya, provided a classic example of this. It is a relic of the vast tropical rain-forests that once swept across the centre of Africa from the Atlantic to the Indian Ocean. Bob Turton went there in the early days to build Rondo Sawmills. In those days he lived rough. One of his staff came to him and said: 'Bwana, we have found an Elgon olive, but it so big it will take a week to cut it down.' Bob was so impressed when he saw it he said: 'This is where I will build my dream bungalow, and that tree will stand in the middle of the lawn, and when my friends come to see me they will gaze upon it in awe.' He did just that. His bungalow was beautiful and his lawns were well cared for. His tree was so big you could have hidden a horse in the space between any of the buttresses in the trunk which supported the massive crown 100ft (30m) above. The tree should have thrived, but when I last saw it the top was becoming stag-headed, and I do not doubt that today it is dead. Was it really sun-scorch, or was it pining for the other forest giants that had once surrounded it?

When the trees are gone, and grass has taken their place, the pattern of animals species changes dramatically. The plains game increases at the expense of that of the forest. And when the grazers are in the majority there can be little or no regeneration of forest trees.

I have mentioned earlier how buffalo were almost extinct at the turn of the century as a result of an outbreak of rinderpest, and how the activities of the Mau Mau and the security forces as they lived off the land prevented any large-scale return. Today, with adequate protection by the National Parks staff, these animals are back in strength. There are mornings at Treetops when it is possible to sit in the lounge and count up to 400 coming to drink before moving off into the denser forest in an endless black line that makes counting easy. It is true that they do leave the area to find other pastures from time to time, and probably to allow the land to rid itself of ticks and other insects such as buffalo flies. They certainly are what Adraan Kortlandt likes to call 'bulldozer herbivores' for they smash down vegetation all around.

Water-buck are another animal that has increased tremendously, as have wart-hogs. Wart-hogs are normally residents of the really dry places, and in some countries where the Muslim population predominates are about the only animals left. Wart-hogs are diurnal animals that love the heat and only large males venture out at night. They usually enlarge the holes of aardvark (ant-bear), into which they retire backwards in order to emerge ready to fight. At Treetops there are virtually no ant-bears, and so at night the wart-hogs retire into the denser of the thickets. Their constant turning around damages the thickets, and wart-hogs must have contributed significantly to the retreat of the forest. A very few wart-hogs occupy culverts under the roads, and a few the blinds at Treetops, where they are a distinct hazard when one is walking near. Often, when walking down to the carpark at dawn, I see their comical faces, sometimes framed by a huge pair of tusks, staring at me from beneath a bush, just before they dash away with tail erect. Woe betide anyone who gets in the way.

About twelve years ago, when tourism was not on the scale it is today, when poaching was serious and staff of the National Parks authority did not have the means to contain it, five camping sites were constructed in the vicinity of Treetops. At that time all users were under the strict supervision of professional hunters and there is little doubt that their presence did indeed keep poachers away. Today the situation is different, and there is little doubt that the camps have indeed contributed to the retreat of the forest.

It is easy to be wise after the event and say that trees for firewood should have been planted along the Park boundaries at the time of their gazettement. Who could have foreseen in 1950 that the world fuel crisis of 1985 would involve not oil but firewood?

The rules of the Kenya National Parks are very clear, and this was quickly brought home when a firm wanted to take flamingo feathers from the shoreline of Lake Nakuru National Park in order to make souvenirs for the tourist industry. *Nothing* must be removed from a National Park without the authority of the Director. Enforcing this simple rule, however, when Parks are big and staff are few in number is far from easy. Yet it cannot be overemphasised how disastrous it is when dead and dying trees are removed from a forest that is intended to remain a true wilderness. Fallen trees and, to a lesser extent, those that are still standing but dead, keep the ground cool when it is hot, warm when it is cold, dry when it is too wet, and moist when it is too dry. They provide shelter from the wind and shade from the sun, and a home for mammals, birds and reptiles. How many people know that the ivory-billed woodpecker in America has become endangered because foresters would cut down dead trees, thus robbing it of nesting sites? If the trees are left for the termites, when they have finally eaten every piece of every dead and rotten branch, and have themselves died, every nutrient in the tree has been returned to the soil. Grazing animals avoid eating the grass growing amongst the branches of fallen trees unless there is a severe drought, and so regeneration of tree seedlings takes place, and by the time the last branch has rotted away at least one will have reached a height above the limits of browsing, and thus become a replacement for the tree that has died. Thus it can truly be said that every fallen tree removed from a National Park is one more nail hammered into the coffin of the forest.

9

NOW THAT BUFFALO NO LONGER BREATHE DOWN THE NECK

During her 1983 walk at Treetops, Her Majesty had asked me where the old path had been and, to my shame, I had only been able to answer with a vague wave of the hand towards a distant part of the forest and tell her it had been on a different alignment. True, over the previous seven years I had asked myself that same question many times. I had even asked people who had been to the old Treetops, and the answer had always been the same: 'Oh I suppose it joined up with the present path somewhere near where the power-house is.' It was not a very satisfactory answer, but no searches in the forest ever revealed depressions indicating a former path, and eventually I had to accept it as the only answer. In addition I had been totally deceived by the old rusty nails in a tree near Treetops, quite over-looking the fact that they must have been put in after the new Treetops was built in 1957. And so eventually I had come to think that nobody really knew, and that the vague answer of somewhere near the old power-house was true.

Soon after Her Majesty's return visit a big storm blew down a giant Cape chestnut tree some 40yd (36m) from the old Treetops site. It was a tree that had already been standing gaunt and dead at the time of her visit, and I can remember hoping that she wouldn't notice that the tree was now dead. I went over to examine this once proud old monarch of the forest. The roots had, over the years, rotted considerably. I noticed, far up the trunk, a couple of rusty nails. Then I saw nearby and lying half rotted into the soil by the actions of white ants, a 20ft (6m) pole. All along that pole, at 1ft (30cm) intervals, were pairs of rusty nails a couple of inches apart. At once the truth hit me—the pole had once been half a ladder, and the nails high up on the great tree had been where it was secured. I then thought of Jim

Mount Kenya as seen from the vicinity of the Outspan Hotel about the year 1927 and taken by an unknown photographer. Speaking of this area Eric Sherbrooke Walker had said, 'It had never previously been inhabited by Man, and there was no question of depriving indigenous people of their land'. Only his boundary fence shows any trace of the works of Man. *(Block Hotels Archives)*

Corbett's little book, and how he had written that, from the foot of the ladder leading into the fig-tree, the path had gone straight for just 40yd (36m) and that at the bend to the left had stood a huge tree, so that he could see no further. This tree was *just* 40yd (36m) from the site of that old fig-tree! I had more than a clue now to the path of yesteryear, I had direction. The old path must have swung sharply to the left and, if I searched hard enough and long enough, I would surely find more nails in more fallen trees. I might even find them in standing trees.

Eagerly I searched the new alignment and sure enough, in an old, rotting tree trunk, long since fallen to the ground, I found another line of rusty nails, and 50yd (45m) further on another. Jim Corbett wrote about a narrow footpath winding up the Treetops Hill from where the old motor track ended, and on to Treetops itself, and he wrote that the distance was 600yd (550m). I now had a true picture of the latter half of that distance. One more set of rusty old nails would be enough, for his 'two miles of a narrow valley' was clear enough. I searched every standing tree and every fallen tree or log but in vain. Evidence of animals was everywhere, and I expected a buffalo to burst out of cover at any moment. I was thankful for my rifle. How I cursed those greedy people who, years ago, had cut down for firewood every tree as fast as it died or was pushed down. Today we are much more strict, for we know the part fallen trees play in the ecology of the forest, but they were once thought to be 'making the forest untidy', and even today I often get tourists asking me why we don't do something about the fallen trees. How many trees bearing nails must have ended up in local fires!

Next day I returned and searched again through every fallen tree and every standing tree in every direction. And then I found what I was looking for—two pairs of nails near the base of a long-dead tree unable to fall because it was held up by its neighbours which were still alive. I was now only 50yd (45m) from a flat area which must surely have been where the cars turned round—the end of the trail for them and the end of the trail for me. I could now answer that royal question: 'Where was the path?'

Then I had a dream. I would protect an area of the old Treetops site by dragging together old tree-trunks, and there I would plant a new fig-tree with others as companions. From the old carpark the path would be reconstructed and tourists would pay to be conducted on a short safari, to be called 'Footsteps of the Queen'. And eventually the area would be protected by a discreet electric fence. With the money thus made the rest of the forest could be saved from the destruction, so apparent, caused by Man's stupidity over the past fifty-two years.

I bought my fig-tree from Gardenia Nurseries just before the rains were due in March, a fine 5ft (1.5m) tree in a polythene pot. But the rains failed completely. In the first half of 1984 there was little more than 1in (25mm) of rain at Treetops, and the ranching country further north had even less. Cattle started to die in their thousands, and in the drier areas wild animals too. It was a strange drought, for the Coast had rains well up to normal, as did the area of Lake Victoria. It was worst in the area stretching from Machakos to the Somalia border. I could not plant my tree, for it would have meant watering it almost every day. Not only was the distance too far but water was in short supply at Treetops itself. Soon my lovely tree, kept in my garden and root-pruned frequently, was 6ft (1.8m) tall and still growing fast.

The Treetops pool dried up. The forest dried up. The elephants came down off the mountain, following their ancient urge to migrate into the foothills of Mount Kenya even though the moat and its electric fence had been there to stop them for some years. They were very hungry, and it was inevitable that sooner or later they would discover how edible the island of papyrus was in the now dried-up pool. It was, in places, nearly 20ft (6m) tall, and it held a colony of some two hundred nesting weaver-birds, but it made no difference—the elephants ate it all up in a few days and nights. We just could not keep them out, though we tried hard. One night, when about half of it was eaten, I was out in the middle of the night, wearing a raincoat over pyjamas and carrying my rifle. A stubborn old bull just could not be chased off until he had had his fill. He would charge me over and over again, and one could not be sure they were mock charges. When I was within 20yd (18m) the din of the protesting birds was terrific. They buzzed around his head like a huge swarm of angry bees; he took no notice but just spat out the nests and babies.

The following night a herd of forty-seven elephants came in and finished off the papyrus the big bull had left. They could be chased out but they were so hungry that they just circled around the back of the building and returned. Immature fledgling weaver-birds were flying all over the place. Some even flew through the open windows of the photographic room. We tried hard to save them but it was hopeless. The herd did not leave until the island was a shambles of broken stems and crushed nests. Then the hyenas moved in and searched through the broken jungle and, when daylight came, the baboons were there searching for anything that was left. And the following night white-tailed mongooses were there, searching for eggs that might have remained unbroken. And when all was quiet, late at night, the bush-pigs moved in, eating even the roots and rhizomes. As the remnants dried and turned yellow they resembled hay, and tourists would ask whether they were food put out for the hungry animals. Eventually not even a wisp remained. It was as though that busy island had never existed. Catastrophies of that kind must have been taking place ever since the world began, but it did not help to be told that tourists had complained, saying: 'Do not let your hunters chase the elephants away.'

The pool had been stocked with 500 tilapia fish a month before the Queen came, and they had prospered, in spite of the prophets of doom who had said that the water would be too saline for them. I had fed them with chopped greens every day I went on duty and again the day I came off, and

Mount Kenya as seen from Treetops in 1957. *(David Keith Jones)*

when, during the drought, the herons finally had a feast on the last fish in the last pool the fish were up to 8in (20cm) long, having grown 6in (15cm) in eight months. It was sad seeing the last ones caught so easily and so relentlessly, without having a chance to swim away, but they can of course be replaced, and it gave me great satisfaction to know that they thrived in the pool. One day, doubtless, we will again watch the kingfishers flashing like jewels with fry in their beaks from a generation not yet born.

When the last fish had been caught, when the last drop of water had gone from the pool, when the last blade of grass had been eaten or had turned brown, when the last leaves had fallen from the trees, the effects of the drought at Treetops became more serious; indeed they became catastrophic. Most of the animals migrated up to the higher parts of the mountain range, where mist ensured a little greenery, but some animals, like the wart-hogs and the solitary old buffalo bulls, do not like to go far, and soon they died and the stench of their bodies permeated Treetops. Predators did not touch the bodies for it was easy to kill the weakened animals elsewhere. In other Parks there were stories of lions teaching their cubs how to kill by taking them up to buffalo almost too weak to stand, let alone fight. Old bulls, with huge horns so massive they could hardly hold them above the ground, looked pathetic. Once they were so proud, and hardened professional hunters hesitated before going near. Now they looked as if a schoolboy armed with no more than a catapult could walk up and push them over. Not many people died of hunger or its related diseases in Kenya, but in neighbouring Ethiopia and in the Sudan horrific stories began to emerge, and even in Kenya the lorries started going out with famine relief to remote villages. Kenya was estimated to have lost 3 million cows, untold numbers of sheeps and goats, and a wildlife population that will take years to recover. Thousands upon thousands of smallholder families, living on plots of 3 or 4 acres (1–1.5ha), lost their all.

When it reached the point where even a colobus monkey lay dead on the path it was decided to take the tourists around the higher parts of the mountains to ensure they saw animals before arriving at Treetops. It was expensive but highly successful, and even leopards were seen on a number of trips. Nevertheless it did not suit all types of visitors, and I can well remember one trip where a man moaned that he could see no point in travelling endless miles through a dry and dusty forest; all *he* wanted to do was to get somewhere he could go to bed and not be bumped around. Treetops is a place of endless frustrations.

As has already been stated, lack of water in the pool has been a curse at Treetops ever since its inception in 1932. It was decided to take advantage of the 1984 drought to deepen the dried-out pool on a scale much more ambitious than had been the case in 1968–9. Heavy machinery was brought in and a depth of 8ft (2.4m) was eventually reached. At that depth, however, and with the surrounding area looking like a moonscape, the huge excavator broke down and could not be used again. Presumably there were no spare parts in the country. Eventually all the heaps of spoil had to be spread by hand. Then the area was planted with grass and watered to the best of our ability, though not until the drought ended was this really effective.

Once I fully understood the problems of how to grow trees at Treetops I got down to the big job of planting my fig-tree on the exact site of the original building where the Queen had spent the night in 1952. I had no illusions about the problems. It would have to be safe from the attentions of up to 100 elephants all bent on its destruction, with maybe three times that number of buffaloes. It has been said that only one 'orthodox' type of fence has kept elephants under control, and many have been tried. That very special fence was around the Addo Bush National Park in South Africa, and it was made from miles and miles of tramlines taken up from Port Elizabeth when that mode of transport became obsolete. They were lashed together with their own own cables. Electric fences are becoming more and more popular but their weakness is that they are only as strong as the current passing through. Not only do power failures occur but when predators are on the move, when big animals are fighting, or when herds are panicking, no mild electric shock will stop them.

During those months of the drought, when it was so dry that I could not possibly plant the tree I had bought, I built my *boma* (fence) around the site of the old Treetops, using the company Land-cruiser to pull together fallen trees from miles around. I vastly underestimated then how big that *boma* would have to be to deter elephants. Buffaloes, and even rhinos, are comparatively easy to fence against but elephants are capable of picking up and tossing away a tree-trunk that needed a dozen men to lift it into place. And sometimes they will do this just for fun. By the time I had enclosed a square chain of logs in circular fashion my staff called it my *manyatta*—the enclosure of thorntrees the Maasai use to protect their village, and into which they herd their cattle at night for safety.

My gardener and I planted the Queen's Fig-tree on 23 August 1984—not because the drought was over, for the end was not even in sight, but because it was becoming so root-bound that I was worried about its survival, and at best it would take a long time to recover. The rains did not come until the first week in October, and until then we had to carry water to it, and to the group of trees we planted around it.

What does it entail, planting a tree in an area as full of wild animals as the vicinity of Treetops? Our experimental plot had taught us a lot but I was still not prepared for the degradation of soil we encountered there. Not only was the 'soil' like cement, totally devoid of a crumb structure, but to dig the holes we had to use crow-bars, dig about 6in (15cm), then fill with water and leave for a few hours before proceeding. Eventually we had a hold 4ft (1.2m) deep and 6ft (1.8m) across. Before returning the soil we added to it a ton of good farmyard manure and droppings of both buffalo and wart-hogs. Elephant dung was avoided. The belief had been expressed that salt in elephant droppings had been one of the major causes of the retreat of the forest. Although I have never believed this I did not want to take chances. The fig-tree by now was about 6ft (1.8m) tall, and had to be planted with extreme care. Protection was provided for it with four stout cedar posts with a wall of split bamboo, lashings of barbed wire, and a barbed-wire hood over the top. Each post had another barbed-wire cap to foil baboon hands and hopefully further deter them by spiking their bottoms.

Eventually, after we had planted the other trees to be companion to the Queen's Fig-tree, to provide the mycorrhiza and the leaf humus, we finished off the stockade inside the square chain of logs. This consisted finally of fifty stout posts with six strands of the best barbed wire, a wall 8ft (2.4m) high of split bamboo spiked at the top to deter baboons, and each side thatched with cypress branches to make its appearance less artificial. It took a long time to complete that wall as most of the work had to be done on my 'off' days with the help of my gardener.

When we were digging the big hole for the fig-tree we came upon a layer of charcoal a few inches beneath the surface, and in that charcoal were nails, screws, splinters of cedar wood, and a rusty bolt such as builders use to join beams together. It was a strange feeling, looking at those silent relics of the 1954 fire, but it was proof, if proof were needed, that we were on the exact site. Those few inches of soil above the charcoal also intrigued me. Had thirty years of rain washed the charcoal down, or had thirty years of wind built up an accumulation of soil over it? Probably it was a combination of both. It reminded me very much of my forestry days in the English Lake District, when I used to walk upon the parade-ground of Hardknott Castle, in the forest of which I was in charge. Two thousand years ago that parade-ground would have been of gravel, and the mountains around would have echoed with the voices commanding marching soldiers—Roman soldiers. Today there is nearly a foot of peat above that parade-ground, and it is desolate and deserted, with only the Herdwick sheep scampering across it. The sheep would have been brought in after the Romans left; for many years only deer would have grazed it.

It is easy to underestimate the intelligence of elephants. A barrier that will keep out ninety-nine will not necessarily keep out the hundredth. Before we had completed the stockade of posts and split bamboo, when the only barrier was the massive great wall of logs pulled into position, a huge bull elephant *did* get through. It was during January 1985, the night of a full moon, and four months after the fig-tree had been planted. I came that night into the viewing lounge at about 11pm, just before going to bed, and could not believe my eyes, for a huge bull was standing right in the centre of the enclosure, a motionless monster just visible in the lights of the lodge.

A few minutes later I was out on the salt-lick, rifle in hand, scattering elephants to right and left with my barking, and very soon I was at the place. But he was not there; no elephants were there. I walked slowly around the enclosure; not a log was out of place. I walked around again. Then I climbed inside. In the moonlight I looked at every tree. Not one had been touched. Puzzled, I climbed out again. Maybe it had been an optical illusion. Maybe he had never actually been inside at all but had been standing just outside. I returned to the building and went to bed. Next morning, when we were due to leave, I went back. In the full light of day I could see where an elephant had balanced on a log a yard across. And inside I found further evidence—footprints on the dusty ground and a pile of elephant droppings. Perhaps he had just wanted to show me what a super-elephant was capable of doing. Next time I came off duty my gardener and I spent a whole day pulling more and more logs around my *manyatta.*

By March my stockade, with its fifty stout posts, barbed wire, split bamboo, and cypress-branch thatching was finished, and I felt we had at long last solved the problem of protecting the Queen's Fig-tree. Then there was another drama. One night, when I was sitting in the Treetops lounge, a big herd of elephants was on the salt-lick. No fewer than sixteen of the huge pachyderms formed a semicircle around the *manyatta* of logs and commenced eating the bush growing between the logs. Then they all stretched out their trunks and appeared to have a competition as to which could stretch the furthest towards the trees. We had calculated that no elephant could stretch its trunk more than 17ft (5m) and on that assumption the trees were safe. But sixteen elephants, averaging 5 ton apiece and standing shoulder to shoulder, can exert a pressure even those tramlines of Port Elizabeth would bend under. And what if one should do a balancing act upon another log in its efforts to gain an advantage over its competitors?

Once again I was out on the salt-lick, rifle in hand, and barking my effective bark. But this time there were at least fifty elephants to dispute my right of way towards that group having fun, and there were a number of mock charges before I could break up the party. Next day Lucas and I again had to spend hours pulling logs together to strengthen the *manyatta*.

In June came another devastating threat to the Queen's Fig-tree. This time it was not from extended elephant trunks but from the mischievous hands of baboons. As every safari park in the world has now discovered to its cost, baboons are not only destructive but are almost impossible to keep out of a chosen area. We had spiked the bamboo. We had put a cap of barbed wire on every tree. But bamboo walls have to be supplied with a ladder to enable workers to get in and out, and trees grow and grow until finally that barbed-wire cap has to come off. We knew that some baboons were bound to get through our defences, just as they had with the experimental plot near the kitchens, but we really thought our trees were now too big for baboons to destroy.

Educated baboons of the kind that hang around Treetops can become incredibly angry when they are thwarted, and also terribly destructive. They are not allowed up on the roof until tea is over, and to ensure this two of the staff are stationed beneath the building, armed with stones and a long stick. When a big dog baboon succeeds in eluding these guards and sees the array of goodies on the long table, and is promptly chased into the refuge of the big pearwood tree hanging over the roof, he gets very angry at being frustrated. He will take hold of a branch in both hands and shake it violently until the whole tree trembles. Just how destructive baboons can become was illustrated some years ago, when a big dog baboon got into a bedroom and found there was nothing to eat, only a grey velour hat lying on the bed. He had been spotted getting through the window, yet, when we burst open the door, all that remained of that hat was a ring of chewed felt on the bed. 'I paid £25 for that hat,' moaned the owner 'and I never had the chance of wearing it.' (The British pound was worth very much more than it is today.)

In the *manyatta* at this time was the Queen's Fig-tree in the centre, with the barbed-wire cap removed from its 9ft (2.7m) high head, but its wall of bamboo and its four cedar posts still in position. Around the perimeter were four cordia trees, four other fig-trees, one Elgon olive tree, and two exotics from the Kakamega forest which had been included simply because of the shortage of trees in the Nursery due to the drought. The cordia trees had all grown at a terrific rate, and equalled the Queen's Fig-tree in size.

PLEASE KEEP THE DOOR LOCKED BECAUSE OF BABOONS

Baboons at Treetops are amusing but precautions against theft must always be taken. *(David Keith Jones)*

Nearly all had had their barbed-wire protection removed because it was considered they were too big for molestation by baboons.

We had spent a long day on maintenance work in the *manyatta*—grass cutting, cultivating, weeding and watering—and, as we left, I had looked back and thought how lovely everything looked, with the big cordia leaves bulging a foot above the bamboo walls. Next day, on duty at Treetops, I could see at a glance through my binoculars that something was wrong in the *manyatta*. The cordia trees appeared to be badly knocked about. I did not think of baboons, and could only imagine that elephant trunks had exceeded the 17ft (5m) we thought they could reach. Next morning, however, my opinions changed when I went over to investigate, for all the cordia had been smashed to the ground yet not a single leaf had been eaten. Some of the stems that had been broken were as thick as the wrist. The fence was intact, and there was a peat pile of baboon dung on the top of the steps.

One can only surmise that the baboon troop watched us as we worked so hard that day, then went to see what edible goodies we had left behind for them. Finding none, they had then taken their revenge on the nearest things they associated with us—the four fast-growing cordia trees. Possibly the Queen's Fig-tree would also have been smashed had it not still been protected by the wall of bamboo and wire up to a height of 3ft (90cm).

The retreat of the forest in the vicinity of Treetops has been caused by many factors since 1932, yet only Block Hotels, the management company operating it for its two Kikuyu owners, has done anything in recent years about trying to arrest it. The National Parks authority has maintained all along that it just does not have any money. Within their financial limits Block Hotels has tackled the difficult, complicated and expensive job of doing what should have been done years ago.

A well-known electric-fencing company was called in to provide advice and estimates, but the costs just could not be absorbed into the normal costs of running Treetops and the plans had to be abandoned. Following this various 'experts' came to give help—farmers, cattlemen, horticulturists and landscape gardeners. Nobody seemed to remember that the art of growing forest trees is invested in a shy and remote breed of men called Foresters.

The first positive effort in reclamation was the enclosing of two 3 acre (1.2ha) areas, one each side of the pool. Fencing was effected with two wires and an earthing wire, and the power was solar. That, of course, would have been all right had some means of storing electricity for use at night been provided but it wasn't. The next expert linked up the power with the mains electricity in the lodge, and from that moment results were seen, though many of the trees planted simply died for reasons outlined earlier. Grazing and browsing was greatly reduced, and soon the bush was more than 6ft (1.8m) high. Three wires are not, of course, sufficient to deter animals intending to enjoy better feeding. If the wires are positioned low animals jump over them; if high then animals quickly learn how to get under or through. It was very amusing to watch tactics. One female bushbuck learned to jump between the wires by positioning herself sideways. At first baboons went under, pressing their chins into the ground as they felt the electricity tingle the hair on the back of their necks. Eventually they learned how to run up the posts without touching wires and then jump off the top. It was remarkable, however, how both elephants and buffaloes avoided the place completely after a few shocks.

In the early months after the fence was installed there were many incidents but none as surprising as the one in which a buffalo bull jumped over the wires one night. Buffalo bulls fight for hierarchy until such time as dominancy has been established. This bull had received a thrashing and was being chased by the victor. It is difficult to imagine a buffalo bull nearly a ton in weight clearing a fence 3ft 6in (1m) above the ground but not only did he clear the wires but he did not disconnect the electricity, and the victor, not in quite the same hurry, received the shock on his nose and galloped away.

Three acres (1.2ha) is quite an area, and by the time the buffalo reached the far side, he too was in less of a hurry, and on receiving his first shock did not try to get out but simply walked round and round inside the fence. He was still walking round in the morning, and his temper by then was not improving. We switched off the current and tried to drive him out but he would not go near the wires, and finally we had to dismantle all one side, not a pleasant job with him so close to us. Hunters at Treetops had a lot of unpleasant jobs getting animals out.

In 1985 funds became available and a professional electric fencing firm is busy building a five-strand fence. I do not doubt that it will be effective, and that eventually trees will grow once more on land where they died nearly half a century ago. And I do not doubt that, when the next terrible drought strikes Kenya in about ten years from now, animals will die near it, unable to migrate to Mount Kenya and forbidden the food so near. For many years now Man has solved one problem only to create many more.

In discussing this vexed problem of how to satisfy an expanding tourist industry yet preserve the environment it would be well to take a leaf out of the book of Tiger Tops Jungle Lodge, in Nepal's Royal Chitawan National Park. Thanks to the widespread use of that wonderful animal the Asiatic elephant as a means of transportation, and the determination of their Director of Wildlife Activities, Dr Charles McDougal, not to use vehicles, electricity or machinery of any sort, coupled with a long rest period during the monsoons, the jungle at Tiger Tops remains intact.

Tiger Tops, since its inception, has stressed in all of its brochures that it will never enlarge. They have, however, built another Tiger Tops in India. *There can never be another Treetops.*

BIBLIOGRAPHY

The Monarchy in Britain, (Central Office of Information, London, 1981)
Queen Elizabeth, J. E. Neale (Jonathan Cape, 1934)
The Modern British Monarchy, Sir Charles Petrie (Eyre & Spottiswoode, 1961)
Brief Lives: Queen Elizabeth, Milton Waldman (Collins, 1952)
A Book of Hatfield, Robert Richardson (Barracuda Books, 1978)
A Guide to Earth History, Richard Carrington (Chatto & Windus, 1956)
Rifts and Volcanoes, Dr Celia Nyamweru (Thomas Nelson (Nigeria), 1980)
Africa, Leslie Brown (Hamish Hamilton, 1965)
Treetops Hotel, Eric Sherbrooke Walker (Rober Hale, 1962)
Treetops, Outspan, Paxtu, Jan Hemsing (Sealpoint Publicity, Nairobi, 1974)
Treetops, Jim Corbett (Oxford University Press, 1955)
Olduvai Gorge, Mary Leakey (Collins, 1979)
The Tree Where Man Was Born, Peter Mathiessen (Collins, 1972)
Kenya Trees and Shrubs, Ivan Dale and P. J. Greenway (Buchanans' Kenya Estate
    Ltd, London, 1961)
The Jungle Tide, John Still (William Blackwood, 1930)
Maneaters of Kumaon, Jim Corbett (Oxford University Press, 1983)
I Walk with Lions, Col Mervyn Cowie (Macmillan, New York, 1961)
Fly Vulture, Col Mervyn Cowie (Macmillan, New York,   )
The Spotted Lion, Kenneth Gandar Dower (Heinemann, 1937)
Out in the Blue, Vivienne De Watteville (The Deveroux Books, 1927)
Out of Africa, (Karen Blixen, Putnam, 1937)
One Life, Richard Leakey (Michael Joseph, 1983)
The Cliff Dwellers of Kenya, J. A. Massam (Seeley Services & Co Ltd, 1927)
Jim Corbett's India, R. J. Hawkins (Oxford University Press, Delhi, 1980)
Empty Highways, R. O. Pearce (William Blackwood & Sons, 1935)
East African Mammals, Jonathan Kingdon (Academic Press, 1971)
The East African Hunters, Anthony Dyer (The Amwell Press, USA, 1979)
Maasai, Cynthia Salvadori and Andrew Fedders (Collins   )
They Made It Their Home, (East African Standard Ltd, Nairobi, 1962)
Pioneer's Scrapbook, The East African Women's League, (Evans Bros, 1980)
Wildlife in Kenya, John Pearson (East African Publishing House, Nairobi, 1967)
The National Geographic Magazine, Vol CX, No 4, October 1956

ACKNOWLEDGEMENTS

Mr D. Musila, Provincial Commissioner, Central Province, Kenya.

Archives of Block Hotels (Management) Ltd, Kenya.

Col Mervyn Cowie, first Director of Kenya's National Parks.

Mr O. M. Mburu, Chief Conservator of Forests, Kenya.

Mr E. Honoré, Chief Conservator of Forests (retired), England.

Maj Grimwood, Chief Game Warden of Kenya (retired).

Mrs Honor Hurly of New Zealand, daughter of Eric Sherbrooke Walker (founder of Treetops).

Mr Jerry Jaleel of Canada (working on a book about Jim Corbett).

Mr Martin Booth of the British Broadcasting Corporation (working on a documentary about Jim Corbett).

Mr Robin Camm, ex Treetops hunter-escort.

Maj Nicholson, ex Treetops hunter-escort.

Mrs Richardson (for information on Nyeri Polo Club).

Mrs Kay Willson, Royal Lodge, Sagana (ex-caretaker).

Mr Ron Nelson of Naro Moru, Kenya (ex Police Crowd Control at Naro Moru).

Mr Amos Wamunya, Secretary of Nyeri Club.

Mr P. H. Rainford, Chairman of Kenya Golf Union.

Mr Brij Mahan, Nyeri Printers (for information on Nyeri Club).

Mr Vir Singh, Aberdare Timber Co (whose father planted the avenue of eucalyptus trees).

Mrs A. Highwood of Kenya (visited Treetops 1953).

Mr Mike Hudson, editor of KPA Newsletter, Australia.

Mr Jerimia Gitonga of Nyeri (for help with Maasai names).

Mrs Jan Hemsing, public relations consultant to Block Hotels 1969–84 (for preliminary editing).

Mr John Cobby, Divisional Forest Officer at Nyeri.

Mr Mickie Fernandes, official of the Nyeri Polo Club.

Jack and Nan Wood of Yorkshire, England (visited Treetops 1952).

Mrs Beverly, Nairobi (for information on Royal Lodge, Sagana).

Mrs B. L. Simpson of Watamu, Kenya (for information on Nyeri Club).

Mr E. H. Milvain of Cheltenham, England (for information on Hatfield House).

Mr R. H. Harcourt Williams, librarian and archivist (for information on Hatfield House).

Mrs Kate Challis of Nairobi (for information on Royal Lodge, Sagana).
Mr Steve Miller of Mombasa (for information on Royal Lodge, Sagana).
Mr Frank Lane of Pinner, England (for information on Hatfield House).
Mrs D. Sheldrick (for information on the Treetops of 1932).
Mr John Hall, Ennasoit Ranch, Kenya.
Mr W. Woodley, Game Warden Aberdares, 1959–63.

INDEX